W9-BTB-485

THE BUILDING OF AMERICA

100 GREAT LANDMARKS

THE BUILDING OF AMERICA

100 GREAT LANDMARKS

ROBIN LANGLEY SOMMER

This edition published by Barnes and Noble, Inc., by arrangement with Saraband, The Arthouse, 752-756 Argyle Street, Glasgow G3 8UJ, Scotland.

2002 Barnes & Noble Books

Library of Congress Cataloging in Publication Data available

ISBN: 0-7607-3380-5

Printed in China

10 9 8 7 6 5 4 3 2 1

EDITOR: Sara Hunt
CONTRIBUTING EDITOR: Simon E. Saunders
PRODUCTION EDITOR: Deborah Hayes
ART DIRECTOR: Nikki L. Fesak

***Page 1**: The Seattle Space Needle*
***Page 2**: The U.S. Capitol Building*

DEDICATED TO THE BUILDERS OF OUR AMERICA, PAST AND PRESENT

Acknowledgments and Photo Credits

Many of the period photographs and architectural diagrams reproduced in this book are from the collection of the Historic American Buildings Survey, established in 1933 to create a record of America's architectural heritage and the Historic American Engineering Record, a similar body that began in 1969 to prepare detailed records of the nation's engineering achievements. These important collections are housed at the Library of Congress and are accessible to the public. The author and editors have found the information and images in these collections invaluable during the preparation for this book. The HABS and HAER photographs and drawings are listed in the illustration credits below, by page number, including their reference numbers. The publisher would also like to thank Simon Saunders, for the "At a Glance" information panels; Simon Smith of inBETWEENspace, for the artwork on the vertical fold-out; Deborah Hayes, for the gazetteer; and Lone Nerup Sorensen, for the index; grateful acknowledgment is also made to the photographers and institutions listed below for permission to reproduce the images on the following pages: ©**Larry Angier:** 137; ©**Mary Liz Austin:** 64–65; ©**Kindra Clineff:** 33, 34–35, 47, 90–91, 122–123, 123r; **Comstock Images:** 70; ©**Ed Cooper:** 1, 6,9,21, 30–31, 51, 75, 116–117, 138–139, 155; **D. E. Cox Photo Library:** 62; ©**Terry Donnelly:** 105, 118, 119, 130, 131–134, 154, 176; ©**Carolyn Fox:** 136; **Hancock Shaker Village, Pittsfield, Massachusetts:** 37; ©**Rudi Holnsteiner:** 72–73, 160–161, 163, 182–183; ©**Kerrick James:** 82–83; ©**Wolfgang Kaehler:** 10, 16–17, 18, 19 (top), 56, 129, 168–169; ©**Balthazar Korab:** 2, 15, 22, 23, 24, 32, 45, 48, 49, 60, 61, 68, 77, 85, 86 (both), 87, 88, 89, 92, 93, 94, 96, 97, 98, 100, 102, 104, 106, 113 (fold-out), 124, 125, 126, 127, 128, 140, 147, 148, 150–151, 152–153, 156, 157, 162, 164, 165, 166, 167, 170, 171, 172, 173, 175, 178, 179, 180, 181; **Library of Congress,** Historic American Buildings Survey/Historic American Engineering Record Collections: 12 (HABS, ILL, 16-CHIG, 60-7); 13 (HABS, FLA, 50-PALM, 5-16, photographed by Jack E. Boucher); 19 (HABS, NM, 28-RANTA, 1-NM7); 20 (HABS, PA, 5 1-PHILA, 6-1430 [top & bottom]); 26 (HABS, ME, 3-CAPEL, 2-123); 28 (HABS, ARIZ, 10-TUCSO.V, 3-13); 29 (ARIZ, 10-TUCSO.V, 3-64, photographed by Donald W. Dickensheets,); 36 & 39 (HABS, MASS, 2-HANC, 9-674); 41 (HABS, MD, 4-BALT, 22-1, photographed by E. H. Pickering,) 42 (HABS, NY, 60-TARY, 1A-73 [top]; HABS, NY, 60-TARY, 1A-NY-5538-A, [bottom] photographed by Jack E. Boucher); 44 (HABS, GA, 26-SAV.V, 1-7); 46 (HAER, MASS, 9-LOW, 7-MA-16); 52, 53, 54-55 (HABS, CAL, 38-ALCA, 1-A-21, 26, photographed by Jet Lowe); 57 (HABS, UTAH, 18-SALCI, 4-1); 59 (HABS, UTAH, 18-SALCI, 2-15 [top]; HAER UT-1 [bottom]; 63 (NC, 28-BUXT, NC-357 [top & bottom]); 66, 67 (HABS, CONN, 2-HARF, 16-13; HABS, CONN, 2-HARF, 16-67, photographed by Jack E. Boucher); 71 (HAER, NY, 31-NEYO, 90-6, photographed by Jack E. Boucher); 74 (HABS, CAL, 12-EUR, 6-9, photographed by Jack E. Boucher [top]; HABS CA-1911 [bottom]); 76 (HABS CA-1958); 78 (HABS, NY, 11-HUD, 1-4, photographed by Cervin Robinson); 84 (HABS, CAL, 19-LOSAN, 11-CA-334); 107 (HABS, ORE, 3-GOCA.V, 1-4, photographed by Marvin Rand); 108, 109 (HABS, IOWA, 97-SIOCI, 3-3, 17, photographed by Jack E. Boucher); 110, 111 (HABS, CAL, 19-LOSAN, 65-3, 10, photographed by Marvin Rand); 114, 115 (HABS, CAL, 14-DVNM, 1-F-25, 15, photographed by Jack E. Boucher); 120 (HABS, GA, 61-ATLA, 2-1[top], 2-2[bottom], photographed by Jonathan Hillyer); 121 (HABS, FLA,13-MIAM,16-1, photographed by Walter Smalling, Jr.); 135 (HAER, CAL, 38-SANFRA, 140-34, photographed by Jet Lowe); 158 & 159 (HAER, MO, 96-SALU, 78-14; 78-34, photographed by Jack E. Boucher); **National Archives:** 8, 40, 52, 58, 113; ©**Paul Rocheleau:** 38, 69, 101, 141, 142, 143, 144, 145, 146; ©**Simon Smith:** 113 (artwork, fold-out); **Union Pacific Museum Collection:** 99; ©**Charles Ziga:** 27, 43, 50, 79, 80–81, 95, 103, 112

Contents

In recent years, interest in American architecture and engineering has mounted steadily, moving from the realm of scholarly studies pored over by professionals and specialists into the wider realm of general readership among "everyday people" who want to know more about our nation's roots and the built landscape that has carried our past into the present. Consciously or not, we are all affected by the places in which we live and work from day to day, which are, in turn, shaped by regional history, climate, culture, natural resources, economy, and other elements including fads and fashions.

Personal preferences are another important factor. Some people enjoy the noise, bustle, and excitement of the city, while the proverbial "country mouse" is happiest on a farm, or in a small rural community where family and neighborhood ties remain strong and people live closely with nature. Midway between is the suburbanite, whose evolution began during the nineteenth century, when new roads, railways, bridges, and tunnels made it possible for breadwinners to commute between city and country. Prosperous businessmen in major cities like Boston, New York, Chicago, and San Francisco could have both elegant townhouses and luxurious country retreats—a practice that the rapid development of the automobile during the early twentieth century facilitated. Similarly, our commercial establishments, houses of worship, government buildings, schools, and monuments have evolved over the centuries to reflect the dynamic growth of a multifaceted, multiethnic nation.

As the respected writer Hugh Morrison reminds us, "In studying architecture, we should learn to read buildings themselves rather than mere words about them." That is why this volume is illustrated not only with a wealth of color photographs, but with a great number of floor plans, diagrams, elevations, and cutaway sections that show the infrastructure of representative landmarks. These features help us to see a given structure from the inside out, as it were, and contribute immeasurably to our understanding of the planning, materials, and purpose for which it was designed.

Building in America began with the native peoples who occupied the continent long before the advent of Europeans. Their pre-Columbian structures include the fascinating ruins of the cliff dwellings seen at Mesa Verde, Colorado, and the rectangular plankhouses still built by Northwestern tribes to this day and ornamented with totemic symbols. The mysterious Mound Builders of the central and eastern United States used both earth-wall and timber construction techniques to build hundreds of burial and temple mounds that have yielded objects as diverse as stone effigies, copper ornaments, pipes, and seashell masks. The Southwestern Pueblo peoples, descendants of the original cliff dwellers, made adobe bricks of mud and straw, plastered with wet mud, to build their multilevel, flat-roofed complexes, as seen at Taos Pueblo, New Mexico, the nation's oldest continuously inhabited community. More ephemeral constructions made by nomadic peoples include the Plains Indian tipi of painted hide stretched over a portable wooden framework and the dome-shaped, reed-covered wickiup used by the hunting and gathering tribes of California and the arid Plateau region.

Some features of these indigenous structures were adapted by European explorers and the colonists who followed

Opposite: *The dwellings in New Mexico's Gila Cliff National Monument date from AD 1250–1350. The people of the Mogollon culture created homes in the cliff's natural caves and crevasses, using stone, mud, and timber.*

them beginning in the early seventeenth century. The Spanish adopted the adobe construction techniques that had precedents in their homeland, while early English settlers on the East Coast dug pits to store food and fashioned crude wooden shelters similar to those of the Eastern Woodlands peoples. Later, as they moved beyond bare survival, the English colonists of New England and Virginia became more widely distributed and built primarily wooden structures influenced by medieval and later precedents in the Mother Country.

***Below:** Children of Spanish origin pose outside an adobe church in New Mexico. In the Americas, the history of building with earth can be traced as far back as 3000 BC, to Peru's Chicama Valley.*

Those in the coastal communities that became major ports soon evolved more sophisticated structures. Many prospered as merchants and planters who modeled their homes and public buildings on the changing fashions of European architecture. Another advantage was that bulky building materials and expensive window glass could be transported by water, as seen in the development of such cities as Boston, Philadelphia, and New York City. In the evolution of the Southern plantation economy, stylistic precedents set in Europe were translated into a new idiom that combined both Caribbean and local influences. Gunston Hall, for example, a Potomac plantation house built in 1758 by the Revolutionary patriot George Mason, a friend and neighbor of George Washington, was influenced by the English architect Sir William Chambers. According to Harry R. Conner, author of *Colonial Homes in the Southern States,* "Chambers shares the honors with Chippendale of adapting Chinese forms and decorative furniture and...adhered to the Anglo-Palladian traditions during the Greek Revival in England.

" The plan of the house is the most common of Colonial types—four rooms to [each] floor with a transverse stair hall....The rooms on the second floor open on each side of a hall which runs at right angles to the hall below and terminates at each gable end of the house. These rooms were small and low-pitched, with dormer windows and wide low window seats. A steep ladder leads up from the hall into the attic. This upper region is lighted and ventilated by a round window in each gable end....The walls are made of red brick laid up in Flemish bond [cut-stone quoins at the corners], in the English late-Renaissance style."

Left: *The Medford Farmhouse, in East Hampton, New York, was built in 1660 and is an example of the Colonial-era saltbox style, characterized by the asymmetrically pitched roof.*

As tobacco, rice, and cotton became increasingly profitable crops with the importation of slave laborers from Africa and the Caribbean Islands, stately plantation houses in both the Jacobean and Classical Revival styles crowned hills overlooking the rivers that transported their products to market. Those who were enslaved often built thatch roofed shelters like the ones they had used in Africa, while frontiersmen and hard-driven small farmers modeled their buildings on the log cabins, or "cribs," first erected by Swedish and German settlers. Since timber was plentiful from the Atlantic Coast to the Mississippi River, it became the principal colonial building material. Dutch settlers of the Hudson River Valley were an exception in that they used mainly brick and stone, while the French, from eastern Canada southward into New England and the Mississippi River Valley, employed both masonry and timber construction techniques.

The Revolutionary War with England had important architectural influences on the new nation, from the simplified Federal style that took precedence over the Georgian to the Greek and Roman Revivals that asserted American adherence to the ideals of pure democracy as expressed in classical antiquity and reinterpreted during the Renaissance. The new national capital at Washington, DC, was carefully planned by a consortium of architects ranging from the French engineer Pierre Charles L'Enfant to the amateur architect William Thornton, Benjamin Henry Latrobe, James Hoban, and a dozen others who have worked on the city's government buildings and monuments down to the present day. All public buildings completed since the Capitol (begun in 1793) and the White House have been designed to complement these two buildings. (An interesting sidelight is the fact that architect Samuel McIntire, who almost won the competition for the design of the Capitol Building, was commissioned by the rich Salem, Massachusetts, shipping merchant Elias Hasket Derby to build a teahouse on his estate.

According to Gwyn Headley, author of *Architectural Follies in America* (John Wiley & Sons, 1996), "McIntire knew the rules, but he played with them rather than by them. He produced a hidden masterpiece, a tiny two-story teahouse with all the classical conventions correctly copied but rearranged with a truly American disregard for convention ....There is no garden building of equal importance in America.")

Even vernacular folk houses like the original New England farmhouse and the Mid-Atlantic log cabin were affected by independence, as growing numbers of original settlers spread from the Allegheny Mountains to the Mississippi River and beyond. Sod houses hewn from the tall-grass prairie appeared on the Great Plains, and the burgeoning Pacific States, from California to Alaska, adapted their built landscape from Spanish Colonial, Native American, and Early American forms transported across the Rocky Mountains and modified to new environments. Immigrants from China and Japan also exerted their influence in the form of pagodas, Zen gardens, and rich fabrics and artifacts for interior decoration.

As a network of steel rails, improved roads, and major engineering projects like the Erie Canal and lighthouses for coastal and inland waterways bound the East and West Coasts together more closely, a series of eclectic styles became more widespread throughout the nineteenth century. Among the most influential was the Gothic Revival style, as seen in stone mansions like Lyndhurst in Tarrytown, New York; the more affordable Carpenter Gothic buildings, with wooden rather than carved-stone tracery; and a host of churches, college quadrangles, even commercial buildings with pointed lancet windows, medieval-style oriels (upper-story bay windows supported by a corbel or bracket), elaborate rooftop finials—even gargoyles like those that served as rain-spouts on European cathedrals. Architect Alexander Jackson Davis was instrumental in popularizing this Romantic, as opposed to Classical, style, along with a host of others that spread rapidly across the country. As Davis noted in his diary, he could design buildings including "English Cottage, Collegiate Gothic Manor House, French Suburban, Switz [sic] Cottage, Lombard Italian, Tuscan from Pliny's Villa at Ostia, Ancient Etruscan, Suburban Greek, Oriental, Moorish, and Castellated"! Obviously, not all of these designs were widely built, but their influence is seen in such estates as Olana, the Persian-inspired Hudson River Valley home of artist Frederick Church, and the endless embellishments of the Queen Anne style, as embraced by Americans at Philadelphia's Centennial Exposition of 1876.

At the same time, the engineering revolution ushered in by ever growing industrialization brought another major development in the second half of the nineteenth century. A much simpler and more functional type of architecture based on iron (later, steel) frameworks began to appear in our cities. Strong, but light, metal framing made it possible to use glass more extensively, and the standardization of structural elements increased the speed and economy of construction. These innovations would culminate in a new aesthetic for tall public buildings—skyscrapers—as pioneered by architect Louis Sullivan and other members of the influential Chicago School, including William Le Baron Jenney, Daniel H. Burnham, and John Wellborn Root.

Opposite: *The cornerstone of America's most famous residence was laid in 1792. President George Washington oversaw construction of the Greek Revival structure but died before its completion. President John Adams and his wife Abigail, arriving in 1800, were the first residents.*

Below: *Chicago's 240-foot Schiller Building was one of the earliest examples of skyscraper design, pioneered by Louis Sullivan. Completed in 1892, the seventeen-story tower, which features a steel skeletal support, was demolished in 1961.*

As Ada Louise Huxtable explains in *The Tall Building Artistically Reconsidered* (Pantheon Books, 1982), "The skyscraper was a response to the growth of cities and business and the concentration of commercial activities housing many people on increasingly congested and expensive urban sites. Its most dramatic technological advance was the quickly erected metal frame and curtain wall. The nonsupporting external façade could be clad at any point; it was no longer restricted to rising slowly and weightily from the ground." Acknowledging Sullivan's visionary mastery of this unprecedented Early Modern form, she adds: "The problem that so many were struggling with in print and practice had already been solved by Louis Sullivan. Translating structure and plan into appropriate form, cladding, and ornament, without dependence on the rules and practice of the past, he had developed what others still sought: a skyscraper style." This is clearly seen in the handsome Wainwright Building of St. Louis, Missouri (1890–91) and the impressive structures that followed upon it before the turn of the twentieth century: Buffalo, New York's, Guaranty Building; the Carson, Pirie, Scott Store in Chicago; and New York City's Bayard Building.

Sullivan's concern with organic form was shared by his disciple Frank Lloyd Wright, who became perhaps the single most influential force on twentieth-century architecture and design. It is interesting to observe that both men were products of the romantic Victorian age, with its wide range of styles, from the popular Italianate and French Empire to the indigenous Stick and Shingle styles and the Romanesque Revival creations of Henry Hobson Richardson. Even as Neoclassicism and other revivals, from Chateauesque to Beaux Arts Eclectic, were having their day—between the 1890s and the 1940s—Wright was breaking new ground, from his early horizontal Prairie-style houses through the "textile-block" concrete buildings of the Southwest and the versatile Usonian dwellings of the 1930s and '40s to the bold essays in rounded and poured-concrete forms, including the Solomon R. Guggenheim Museum in New York City, completed in 1959 when death ended his remarkable seventy-year career.

Skyscrapers continued to reach new heights during the Early Modern period, when Art Deco had an impact on such "cathedrals of commerce" as William Van Alen's Chrysler Building (1930), with its setbacks, chevrons, and stylized decorative motifs that paid homage to the automobile age—all clad in gleaming stainless steel and crowned by a tall spire that emphasized the vertical thrust of the building. It was soon followed by the landmark Empire State Building, which soared even higher at the record-setting rate of four-and-a-half stories per week. Art Deco, with its streamlined forms, rounded windows, and distinctive, colorful ornamentation, also enjoyed several decades of popularity as a residential and commercial style, notably along Florida's Miami Beach, where many of the resort's distinctive hotels have been restored to their former glory in recent years.

The 1930s also saw an unprecedented feat of American engineering: the Golden Gate Bridge that spans the entrance to San Francisco Bay. Designed by chief engineer Peter Strauss, it is a long, thin, and flexible suspension span anchored by the tallest towers of any bridge in the world. Its length of 4,200 feet also set a record—that of spanning an expanse far greater than any previously attempted.

The German-born architects Walter Gropius and Ludwig Mies van der Rohe, both of whom emigrated to America when the Nazi Party came to power in their homeland, brought with them the clarity, symmetry, and precision they had espoused in the quest for pure form exemplified by the Bauhaus—the school of design founded by Gropius in Dessau in 1919. This was a new way of stating the principles of Sullivan and Wright—that a building's form should follow its function and that the structure itself should show through. The Bauhaus was built mainly of glass, steel, and concrete—all materials that would remain paramount when these distinguished architects made their contributions to the building of America. Their influence was widely felt, as Gropius became head of Harvard University's Graduate School of Design, and Mies van der Rohe was commissioned to design the campus for Chicago's Armour Institute (later the Illinois Institute of Technology). From 1939 until 1958, he designed many other notable Modern buildings, including Chicago's Lake Shore Apartments (1951) and New York City's imposing Seagram Building (1957), built of bronze and glass and raised on great piers over an open space. It has had countless imitators across the country. The philosophy shared by Gropius, Mies, Rudolph Schindler, Marcel Breuer, and others was first called the International Style in 1932, when historian Henry Russell Hitchcock and future architect Philip C. Johnson published their landmark book of the same

Above: *The Art Deco-style Paramount Theater in Palm Beach, Florida (1926), was one of the last theaters designed especially for the viewing of silent movies. Designed by Joseph Maria Urban, such Moorish influences as the ogee arch above the entrance and dome toward the rear no doubt derive from his earlier work in Egypt and Russia.*

Opposite: *The stunning atrium of Atlanta's Hyatt Regency Hotel, with its distinctive glass capsule elevators, spawned a thousand imitations and inspired one of the most coveted architectural prizes, the Pritzker* *(see page 165).*

name, predicting that the new style would establish itself around the world.

In the United States, many major architects were influenced by the International Style, including Louis Skidmore, Nathaniel A. Owings, and John Ogden Merrill, who formed the partnership of Skidmore, Owings and Merrill (SOM) in 1939. They were responsible for such notable structures as New York City's Lever House (1952), Chicago's John Hancock Center (1970), and the world's tallest building, the Sears Roebuck Tower (1974), soaring to a height of 1,470 feet, with 4.4 million square feet of floor space. In 1962 SOM won the first Architectural Firm Award of the American Institute of Architects (AIA).

Philip C. Johnson was an authority in American architecture as a writer, lecturer, and critic even before he took his degree at Harvard University in 1943, at the age of thirty-seven. The glass house he designed for himself in New Canaan, Connecticut (1949), was instrumental in furthering his reputation. Intimately involved from the outset with New York City's influential Museum of Modern Art, he added two wings to the building (1950 and 1964) and designed its sculpture garden in 1953. His projects are sophisticated and boldly conceived, as seen in the Crystal Cathedral of 1980 in Anaheim, California, designed during his twenty-year partnership with John Henry Burgee. They also designed the twin towers of Pennzoil Place in Houston, Texas (1976). Johnson's high profile as an architect, writer, and lecturer helped to advance the careers of a new generation, including Michael Graves, Robert A.M. Stern, and Peter Eisenman.

Both native-born and émigré architects have continued to make a powerful impression on the American landscape in their own ways, progressing from Late Modernism on to Postmodernism and beyond. Cesar Pelli, from Argentina, established a thriving practice—still growing—that is responsible for the elegant Pacific Design Center in Los Angeles, begun in 1975, and for the impressive Norwest Center (1989) in Minneapolis, which represents a transition from Late Modernism into materials and forms that are more responsive to historic buildings of the early twentieth century. Richard Meier, who acknowledges Le Corbusier and Frank Lloyd Wright as his major influences, designed the widely admired High Museum of Art in Atlanta, Georgia, with its central sky-lit atrium and curving ramps that provide access to the upper floors. Born in Shanghai, architect I.M. Pei studied at Harvard and became involved in large-scale urban projects that reflect his belief that architecture can be monumental without being impersonal, as evidenced by the Holocaust Museum in Washington, DC (1993). Minoru Yamasaki, born in Seattle to Japanese immigrants, designed more than eighty-five important buildings before his death in 1986, including the Reynolds Metal Company Building in Detroit (1960), the Federal Science Pavilion for the World's Fair, Century 21, in Seattle (1962), and, with Emory Roth, New York City's World Trade Center (1973), catastrophically destroyed on September 11, 2001, in the worst terrorist attack in American history.

As the new millennium begins to unfold, we can be certain of one thing—that talented, enterprising, and visionary men and women will continue to contribute ever more widely to the building of America and to the influence of its master builders on other nations in the common cause of international understanding, cooperation, and solidarity.

"The boy cried and cried. The blood came out, and finally he died. With his tears our lakes became. With his blood the red clay became. With his body the mountains became, and that was how Earth became."

—Taos Pueblo creation story

"WE ARE IN ONE NEST"

This multistory adobe complex, with its protruding roof timbers called vigas, has changed little in design in almost a thousand years. The protective coating of mud that maintains the integrity of the adobe-brick construction is renewed regularly by hand in the time-honored way, and the multigenerational families who live here have conceded little to the incursions of other cultures, beginning with the advent of Spanish conquistadors around 1598.

The arid lands of the lower Rio Grande Valley, where some 50,000 Pueblo peoples lived in riverside communities like Taos, did not become a magnet for Spanish conquest from Mexico until rumors of gold and silver here brought both soldiers and Franciscan missionaries to what is now New Mexico. What they found was not the pre-

Below: *Taos Pueblo has remained virtually unchanged for almost a millennium.*

cious metals they sought, but one of the most sophisticated native cultures in North America. Unlike the nomadic Southwestern tribes, the Pueblo peoples were sedentary farmers who cultivated corn, squash, and beans in the fields below their mesa-based dwellings. Their "apartment-house" villages had terraced rooms, so that the roofs of the lower rooms formed porches for those above. Originally, Taos Pueblo and others had few doors or windows: people entered a room by climbing a ladder to the roof, then entering a roof hole by another ladder. In time of war, all the ladders could be pulled up to turn the dwelling into a fort, where stores of water and dried staples were kept. Such access ladders are still in use for moving from one story to another, and to descend into the underground ceremonial chambers called kivas.

AT A GLANCE: TAOS PUEBLO

- The Taos Puebloans are believed to have lived here for nearly 1,000 years, making this the nation's oldest continuously inhabited community.
- Despite opening their community to visitors, the people of Taos have kept their traditional lifeways largely intact: remarkably little has changed here since Coronado first encountered the Pueblo peoples in 1540.
- The two structures comprising the Pueblo, *Hlauuma* and *Hlaukwima* (north and south houses), currently house approximately 150 residents, who eschew such conveniences as electricity and running water, remaining faithful to many of their ancient traditions.

Oppression by the Spanish finally led to the unsuccessful Pueblo Revolt led by Popé in 1680, and many Indians pretended to convert to Christianity while maintaining their traditional beliefs. The Spanish used enforced labor to subdue the Pueblo peoples, but they clung to their lifeways with remarkable tenacity. When the United States seized this region in the Mexican War of 1846–48, many promises were made and broken, but Taos became a major Southwestern culture center because of the skill of its craftsmen and the stark beauty of its landscape, which attracted such artists as painter Georgia O'Keeffe and photographer Ansel Adams. Today, Taos maintains its proud place as the oldest continuously inhabited community in the nation.

AT A GLANCE: THE ALAMO

- The *Misión San Antonio de Padua* was authorized by the Spanish Duke of Valero, viceroy of Mexico, in 1716 and established in 1718 as *San Antonio de Valero* in his honor. Its cornerstone was laid in 1744.

- The missionaries abandoned the church in the early 1790s, and it was used as a military stronghold from the early 1800s.

- The name Alamo was given to the mission around 1807, by Spanish militia of *La Segunda Compañía Volante de San Carlos* (The Second Flying Company of San Carlos) from Álamo de Parras, Coahuila, Mexico. *Álamo* is Spanish for cottonwood, sparking a legend that the fortress took its name from a grove of trees planted nearby.

"I shall never surrender or retreat... Victory or Death."
—William B. Travis

REMEMBER THE ALAMO! Founded by Franciscan missionaries in 1744, this historic fortress was originally the Spanish Colonial-style Church of San Antonio de Valero, located in what is now San Antonio, Texas. The mission consisted of a monastery and church enclosed by high walls.

Over time, it was secularized and occasionally used as a fort by American settlers in the area. (The word *Alamo* is from the Spanish for the cottonwood trees that surrounded the mission.) The famous battle that took place here began on February 23, 1836, after the people of Texas severed their relations with Mexico and sought to become independent. In response, Mexican general Antonio Lopez de Santa Anna advanced upon San Antonio with an army of some 5,000 men. The city had a force of about 150 fighters, commanded by Lieutenant Colonel William Barret Travis. It included several legendary frontiersmen, among them, James Bowie and Davy Crockett. Surprised by the Mexican advance, this small party retreated to the Alamo with the avowed intention "never to surrender or retreat." By March 5, the garrison could not return Mexican fire because its ammunition had run out, and Santa Anna's soldiers scaled the walls and killed the defenders to a man. The battle cry "Remember the Alamo!" became the impetus behind the successful battle for the independence of Texas led by General Sam Houston in April 1836.

When Texas joined the United States in 1846, the U.S. Government leased the Alamo from the Catholic Church and renovated the entire building, adding the façade seen here in 1850.

"Anyone who doesn't feel the crosses simply doesn't get that country."
—Georgia O'Keeffe

STAR OF THE DESERT

In northern New Mexico, time-honored building traditions dictate the use of adobe bricks made from a mixture of sun-dried clay, sand, silt, water, and straw. The chopped straw is a vital ingredient, as reflected in the local proverb *Un adobe sin paja es un adobe sin alma* (An adobe without straw is an adobe without soul). The entire structure, with its timber ceiling beams, is then covered with wet mud, which must be renewed every year to protect the 30-pound bricks from deteriorating. In Ranchos de Taos, established long before Columbus made his first voyage in 1492, indigenous construction by the Southwestern pueblo peoples was adapted by Spanish settlers, who had used a similar style in their homeland.

The famous church of San Francisco de Asis, painted and photographed by a host of gifted artists, is recoated with mud plaster every year in June by the whole community, which celebrates its Hispanic heritage by preserving this revered house of worship. Similar "mudding events" are held in other long-established communities of the region, including La Cueva and Upper Rociada.The walls of the church are four feet thick, and the building is reinforced with large, rounded buttresses, as seen in the rendering below.

AT A GLANCE: THE MISSION CHURCH, RANCHOS DE TAOS

- The Mission Church at Ranchos de Taos is possibly the most photographed in the nation. Its aesthetic grandeur has attracted the eye of numerous world-famous artists, including painter Georgia O'Keeffe and photographer Ansel Adams.

- Ranchos de Taos was settled by the Spanish in 1716. The church building was completed in 1815 by the Franciscans on the site of the community's earlier church.

- The adobe structure is Latin cruciform and is 35 feet wide and 125 feet long. Huge buttresses support the four-feet-thick walls against erosion. The exterior is repainted during an annual public festival with a sand-and-water mixture, applied with sheepskins.

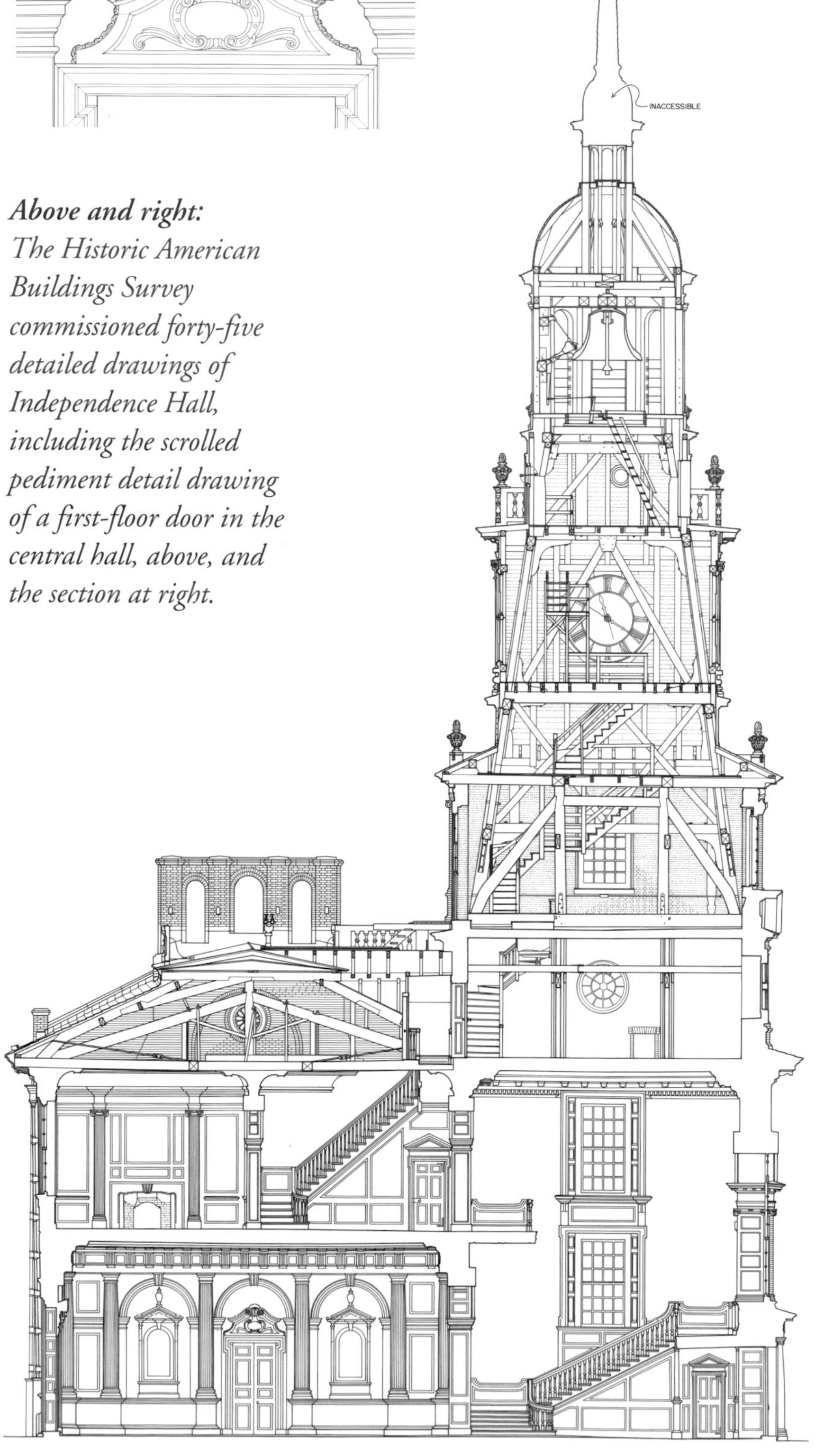

Above and right: *The Historic American Buildings Survey commissioned forty-five detailed drawings of Independence Hall, including the scrolled pediment detail drawing of a first-floor door in the central hall, above, and the section at right.*

MEETING PLACE OF THE FOUNDERS

This stately Georgian building was originally constructed to serve as the State House of William Penn's colony of Pennsylvania, which was a model of religious tolerance and honorable relations with the Native Americans in the region. The schematic diagram at left depicts the hall's central tower and one of the two parallel wings illustrated on the opposite page. The doorway-arch detail, with its ornate broken lintel and classical garland surmounted by a keystone arch based on columns or pilasters, is typical of this style, which originated in England. Other features of Georgian architecture reflected here are its balanced, symmetrical proportions, center-hall floor plan, and multilevel square tower surmounted by a polygonal cupola. The tripart Palladian window over the central entrance (opposite) is also typical of this building style, which was a model for numerous government buildings, churches, schools, and mansions during colonial times.

After the English Quaker William Penn founded Philadelphia (from the Greek for "brotherly love") in 1682, it quickly became the largest city in the American colonies and was nicknamed "the City of Brotherly Love." By 1760 it had surpassed Boston as the largest colonial port and manufacturing center. Soon after, it would become the birthplace of the United States, because of the fact that its state house was the venue for the signature of the nation's founding documents: the Declaration of Independence (1776), whose passage was rung out by the famous Liberty Bell; the ratification of the Articles of Confederation in 1781, and the drawing up of the U.S. Constitution in 1787. During most of the Revolutionary War, Philadelphia served as the capital of the nascent United States.

"I am filled with deep emotion at finding myself standing here, in this place, where were collected together the wisdom, the patriotism, the devotion to principle, from which sprang the institutions under which we live."
—President Abraham Lincoln

What is now Independence Hall National Park, at the eastern end of Market and Chestnut Streets, includes Independence Hall; Congress Hall, where Congress met from 1790 to 1800; and Carpenters' Hall, where the first Continental Congress met. Thus Philadelphia, capital of the aptly named "Keystone State," has been a place of patriotic pilgrimage for generations.

AT A GLANCE: INDEPENDENCE HALL

- Originally built as the colony of Pennsylvania's State House, this landmark was constructed between 1733 and 1756.
- Independence Hall is the site of the signing of America's historic founding documents: the Declaration of Independence in 1776; the ratification of the Articles of Confederation that created a provisional government in 1781; and the creation of the United States Constitution in 1787.
- In 1865, following his assassination, President Abraham Lincoln's funeral cortège stopped here en route to its final resting place in Springfield, Illinois.

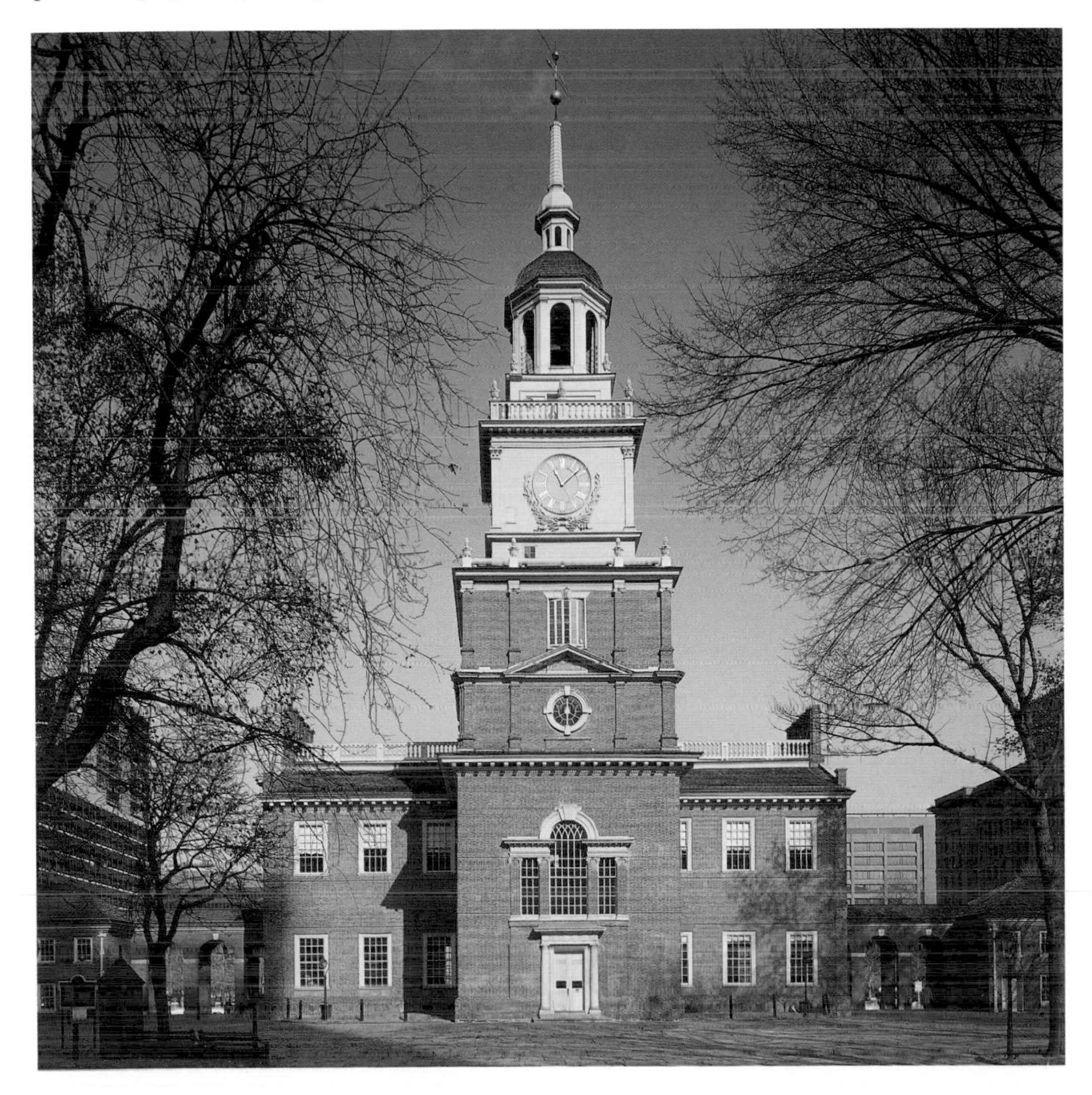

"The passage of the Patowmac [sic] through the Blue Ridge is perhaps one of the most stupendous scenes in nature."
—Thomas Jefferson

AT A GLANCE: MOUNT VERNON

- When George Washington inherited Mount Vernon in 1761, the estate comprised 2,000 acres. By the time of his death in 1799 he had increased its size to 8,000 acres, on which five working farms were established.

- The 9,000-square-foot mansion is 93 feet long and 32 feet wide, excluding its porch. Many of its features were designed by Washington himself, including the two-story piazza overlooking the Potomac.

- The hexagonal cupola serves as an elementary air-conditioning system, its windows providing additional airflow to the building's upper floors. It was added after the Revolutionary War and is topped by the "Dove of Peace," a weathervane commissioned from Joseph Rakestraw of Philadelphia.

ESTATE OF THE UNION

More than 1,000,000 tourists visit the home of our first president every year. Mount Vernon's status as a place of pilgrimage exceeds even the beauty of its architecture, which was inspired in part by the Renaissance architect Andrea Palladio, whose *Four Books of Architecture* (1581) were instrumental in creating the Georgian style in England.

Washington modified Palladian ideas to suit the practical concerns of a Southern gentleman farmer. Wood cladding, for example, was milled to look like stone, and numerous outbuildings and connected dependencies were added over the years. The estate's most impressive architectural feature is the imposing two-story porch overlooking a bend in the Potomac River (added 1787). This square-columned loggia, with its symbolic division between public and private space, has made Mount Vernon the most widespread model for building in the United States.

"And our own dear Monticello, where has nature spread so rich a mantel under the eye."

—Thomas Jefferson

AN ESSAY IN ARCHITECTURE

Monticello (from the Italian for "little mountain") bears the imprint of Thomas Jefferson's years abroad as a statesman and amateur student of architecture. Andrea Palladio and ancient Roman models are combined in the elegant façade of the house in the form of Doric columns, a Roman dome, and the symmetrical wings that project to embrace the spacious lawn. In exploring Classical sources, Jefferson opened a new aesthetic path for the nation, setting American architecture free of domination by the prevailing English Georgian style.

AT A GLANCE: MONTICELLO

- Monticello, home of Thomas Jefferson, was redesigned and rebuilt extensively between its initial construction in 1769 and Jefferson's death in 1826. The house was originally designed with fourteen rooms but by the time it was completed, fifty-six years later, it extended to thirty-three.
- The house is full of labor- and space-saving devices designed by Jefferson himself. His bed was situated in an alcove between the bedroom and the study, giving access to either room. At the foot of the bed was a closet containing a "turning-machine" from which clothes could be selected with ease.
- An avid horticulturalist, Jefferson transformed the surrounding grounds of the estate into a botanical and kitchen garden. Eight acres of land were assigned to 170 varieties of fruit, and the 1,000-foot garden terrace was home to 250 varieties of vegetable.

> *"We have built no temple but the Capitol. We consult no common oracle but the Constitution."*
>
> —Rufus Choate

THE NATION'S CAPITOL

The heart of Washington, DC, is the United States Capitol, the city's geographic and governmental focal point. At night, its glowing white dome, topped by the statue of Freedom, rises 300 feet above the Capitol Plaza. The 20-foot statue was designed by sculptor Thomas Crawford and raised to the dome in 1863.

George Washington laid the cornerstone for the building in 1793, when its design was the work of amateur architect and physician William Thornton, who founded the U.S. Patent Office. His Classical plan had been chosen from a field of seventeen entries, judged by a panel of three commissioners. When Thornton proved unqualified to construct the building as designed, the French architect Stephen Hallet, the runner-up, was employed. Hallet was the second of nine architects to work on the building, which has been enlarged, modified, and rebuilt entirely after it was burned by the British during the War of 1812. The five-story building now covers more than 3 acres, and multimillion-dollar expenditures have been made on the Capitol and its park-like grounds since its inception. With the White House, it has served as the model for all other public building in the capital city; in 1910 Congress created the Commission of Fine Arts to control the artistic aspects of all such public works.

Stately Corinthian-style columns and pilasters decorate the east front of the Capitol. The building's grand central portico measures 160 feet wide. A massive bronze door designed by Randolph Rogers leads into the Great Rotunda, 96 feet in diameter. Historically, John Trumbull's paintings of the Revolutionary War hang on the Rotunda's walls. Two smaller domed rooms, one on either side, are called the North and South Small Rotundas, respectively. The North Small Rotunda is the oldest part of the Capitol.

The room to the north of the Great Rotunda served as the Supreme Court chamber from 1860 to 1935, when architect Cass Gilbert's Supreme Court Building was completed. The Senate chamber is beyond the old Supreme Court chamber, in the north wing of the building. Statuary Hall is in the room to the south of the Great Rotunda, and the House of Representatives meets in the south wing. The Capitol's most recent addition is the work of Hugh Newell Johnson, who studied architecture with Louis I. Kahn and Philip Johnson. His respectful addition has a glass-roofed corridor that leads to offices below grade, reflecting his belief that "Good restoration should never show the hand of the restoring architect."

AT A GLANCE: THE UNITED STATES CAPITOL

- Self-trained architect Dr. William Thornton won the competition for the Capitol Building's design in 1792 following the dismissal of Pierre Charles L'Enfant, the city planner for Washington, DC. President George Washington complimented Thornton's design for its "grandeur, simplicity, and convenience."
- Nine Architects of the Capitol, including Benjamin Henry Latrobe and Charles Bulfinch, worked on the building.
- The structure's most impressive external feature is its gleaming white dome, beneath which lies the huge Rotunda, a circular room 180 feet high and 96 feet in diameter.

AT A GLANCE: PORTLAND HEAD LIGHT

- Merchants of the District of Maine petitioned for the Portland Head Light in the late 1780s, following the deaths of two people in a shipwreck at what is now known as Cushing Island.
- Insufficient funds delayed work on the lighthouse, but it was completed in 1791 after Congress assumed authority for the nation's lighthouses, and federal funding financed its completion.
- The Light has featured in the work of artists, poets, and countless photographers. Longfellow was said to have regularly composed poetry at the site, and Edward Hopper painted it in 1927.

"Steadfast, serene, immovable, the same,
Year after year, through all the silent night
Burns on forevermore that quenchless flame,
Shines on that inextinguishable light."
—Henry Wadsworth Longfellow, "The Lighthouse"

"Portland Head and its light seem to symbolize the State of Maine—rocky coast, breaking waves, sparkling water and clear, pure salt air."
—Edward Rowe Snow

"THAT QUENCHLESS FLAME"

Virtually synonymous with the rugged coast of Maine, this landmark lighthouse was among the first built after the creation of a federal "Lighthouse Establishment" in charge of lighting the young nation's coasts. The 73-foot tower was built with fieldstone, dragged laboriously to the site by teams of oxen, and was originally lit by sixteen lamps filled with whale oil, which first shone out over the waters off Cape Elizabeth in 1791. The light was a godsend to mariners negotiating the dozens of islands in Casco Bay, which extends some 20 miles to Bald Head.

In 1855 the Lighthouse Board had the tower lined with brick and installed a spiral staircase of metal to aid the work of the keepers who maintained the site and its outbuildings, including the fog signal so necessary on this northeastern coast.

At this time, a powerful fourth-order Fresnel lens replaced the oil lamps, representing a great savings in labor for the keepers formerly taxed with the maintenance of the glass lantern that had been continuously obscured by smoke and soot. During the Civil War, the tower's height was raised to 95 feet in the face of sporadic Confederate raids into Portland Harbor, which necessitated better visibility for Union ships that patrolled it.

In 1886 the three-masted bark *Anna C. Maguire* was shipwrecked off the coast, but lighthouse keeper Joshua Strout and his son Joseph risked their lives to rescue all twenty of the people aboard. In these days before the automation of lighthouses, countless families like the Strouts kept their posts for generations and performed heroic service both in keeping the "quenchless flame" burning and rescuing the survivors of shipwrecks. The historic and frequently photographed light at Portland Head is now a fixture of Maine's popular Fort Williams State Park.

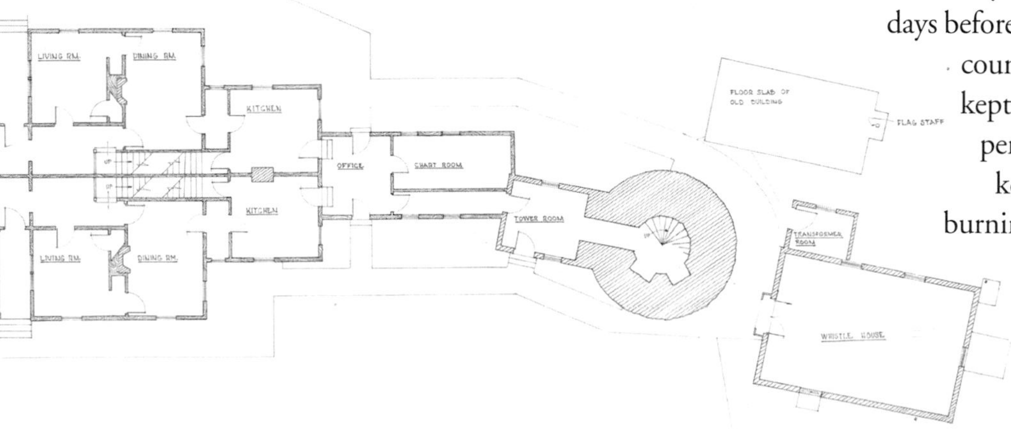

AT A GLANCE: SAN XAVIER DEL BAC MISSION

- A mission was founded at the Pima village of Bac in 1692 by Jesuit Father Eusebio Francisco Kino, but the small church was destroyed in the mid-1700s.
- In 1797 the present structure was completed after fourteen years of labor. The building's missing tower remains an unsolved mystery; theories include the death of a worker whose colleagues subsequently refused to re-enter the tower, and lack of funds for its completion.
- Recent renovators have turned to ancient methods for inspiration. A centuries-old formula for porous mortar using juice from the prickly pear cactus allows moisture to escape from the structure before causing permanent damage.

A REGAL PRESENCE

Master mason Ignacio Gaona, believed to be a native of the Mexican city of Queretaro, is the architect of record for this exemplar of the High Baroque style developed in New Spain during the eighteenth century. The builder was Pedro Bojourquez, with direction from members of the Franciscan Order of Friars Minor. A host of anonymous laborers and artisans, including the indigenous O'odham who would worship here as converts, dug clay for the bricks, shaped and fired them, and laid them in lime mortar to form the walls and multi-domed ceiling. Rocks were hauled to the site for the foundations and inner core of the walls, which rose between 1783 and 1797 at the behest of Franciscan missionaries based in what was then the Mexican Province of Sonora.

"Mission San Xavier del Bac is to southern Arizona what the Grand Canyon is to northern Arizona."
—Senator Barry Goldwater

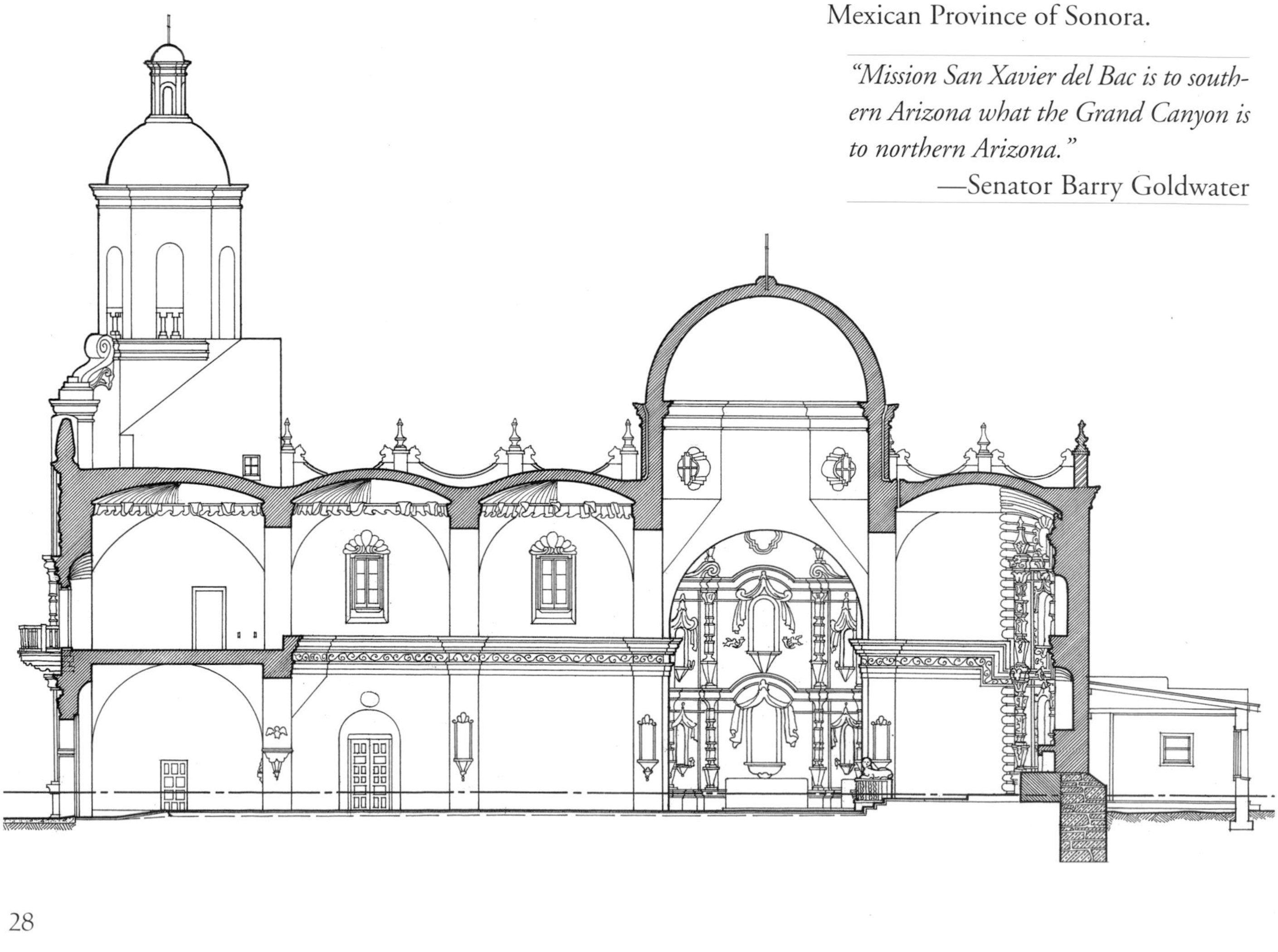

Above: *The eloquent three-story narthex of the church is one of its most impressive features.*

Opposite: *A detailed cross-section of the historic mission.*

Overleaf: *Curvilinear walls, domes, and towers of dazzling white make San Xavier del Bac appear almost miragelike in its desert setting.*

The mission complex includes a single-story convent, a mortuary chapel, and the harmonious church, with its elegant pulpit, choir loft, and narthex. Materials of construction throughout include stone, burned brick with cement plaster overlay, vigas (ceiling beams) of mesquite logs, molded and painted plaster, and pine flooring. The Historic American Building Survey published by the Library of Congress reports that "Under the stimulus of the missionary activities of the padres, agriculture thrived, stock-raising was established, and many Indians were converted to Christianity. The mission reached its height in the period c. 1797 to 1810. With secularization of the Missions in 1813, San Xavier became little more than a parish church.... Not until 1857 did priests again come to San Xavier regularly."

Fortunately, nearby residents—native, Anglo, and Hispanic—retained their loyalty to the historic place of worship, which was deteriorating rapidly by the early twentieth century. The establishment of the nonsectarian volunteer organization Patronato San Xavier in 1978 raised extensive funds and rallied the efforts of all concerned to carry out the faithful restoration that we see today.

IN HONOREM
INDORVM

AT A GLANCE: MASSACHUSETTS STATE HOUSE

- Architect Charles Bulfinch drew inspiration from Somerset House in London, England. So successful and widely acclaimed was his work on the Massachusetts Capitol that he later became Architect of the U.S. Capitol.
- Boston's Beacon Hill, named for its mast upon which a tar bucket would be lit in the event of attack, was partially excavated to create the site for the new building.
- The State Capitol's wooden dome, originally topped with rolled copper by Paul Revere, was gilded with 23-carat gold leaf in 1874, ensuring a corrosion-proof shine.

"During the many years [Bulfinch] presided over the town government, he improved its finances, executed the laws with firmness, and was distinguished for gentleness and urbanity of manners, integrity and purity of character."
—Josiah Quincy,
second mayor of Boston

A GOLDEN AGE

The gifted Charles Bulfinch (1763–1844) is considered the first native-born American architect. He grew up in Boston, Massachusetts, and graduated from Harvard University. A European tour impressed him with the spirit of Neoclassical buildings, and he returned

Right and opposite: *Symbols of Boston, past (the Old State House, opposite) and present (right).*

to Boston determined to make his native city a model of good planning and aesthetic design. First as a selectman, then as superintendent of police, he impressed other city fathers with his ideas and soon became a notable architect in the Federal style embraced by the new United States. He designed row houses, mansions, and public buildings, the best-known of which is this elegant, porticoed state capitol, with its radiant golden dome, completed in 1797. Bulfinch is generally considered the major architect produced by New England to the present day.

STATE OF INDEPENDENCE

> *"Then and there the child independence was born."*
> —President John Adams

This historic Georgian statehouse (right) served as government headquarters during colonial times. The Declaration of Independence was read from its balcony before a large crowd in 1776. At this time, Boston had about 15,000 residents and rivaled Philadelphia as the political and cultural center of the American colonies. Now surrounded by high-rise buildings, the Old State House is a museum, visited by thousands who walk the city's proudly named Freedom Trail. Other shrines along this patriotic pilgrimage include the house of Paul Revere (1670—the city's oldest); the Old North Church, in whose steeple two lanterns signaled that the British were marching toward nearby Concord for the initial battle of the Revolutionary War; and the Granary Burying Ground, the final resting place of John Hancock, Samuel Adams, Paul Revere, and all the victims of the Boston Massacre of 1770.

AT A GLANCE: OLD STATE HOUSE, BOSTON

- Built in 1712–13 to house the government of the Massachusetts Bay Colony, and originally known as the Second Town House (the first was destroyed by fire in 1711), the Old State House is America's earliest extant public building of Georgian design.
- In 1776, upon the Declaration of Independence, the British Crown Lion and Unicorn statues were removed from the building and burned, symbolizing renunciation of colonial rule. King Street was rechristened State Street, the name it carries to this day.

AT A GLANCE: FANEUIL HALL

- Named for Boston merchant Peter Faneuil, who donated the building to the city, the structure at the heart of historic Boston replaced an earlier version that was built by John Smibert in 1742 and virtually destroyed by fire in 1761.
- Charles Bulfinch, creator of Boston's State House (page 32), increased only the height and width of the building during his 1806 renovation, retaining the existing walls.
- Faneuil Hall's second-floor meeting room is known as the "Cradle of Liberty," having witnessed moving protest speeches by such freedom fighters as Samuel Adams, Lucy Stone, William Lloyd Garrison, and Frederick Douglass.

THE CRADLE OF LIBERTY

An enduring exemplar of Old Boston, with its great Doric columns fronting a massive colonnade, Faneuil Hall is also known as Quincy Market. It was donated to the city by the wealthy merchant Peter Faneuil to serve as a central food market catering to international shipping and trade, as well as a public meeting space for town gatherings. The lower levels were leased for market purposes, and the second-floor meeting room became the venue for spirited—sometimes violent—debate that would help to precipitate the American Revolution. Here Samuel Adams and the Sons of Liberty urged influential Bostonians to assert their independence, and reports spread throughout nearby colonies, earning the building its place on the Freedom Trail as the "Cradle of Liberty." Boston's renowned architect and city planner Charles Bulfinch increased the size of the building in 1805, and its reputation as a forum for notable

> *"I expect to plead not for the slave only, but for suffering humanity everywhere. Especially do I mean to labor for the elevation of my sex."*
>
> —Lucy Stone

Right: *The marketplace at historic Faneuil Hall is today a major attraction as the hub of Boston's most vibrant downtown neighborhood.*

freedom fighters like feminist Lucy Stone and abolitionists William Lloyd Garrison and Frederick Douglass endures to the present day, while the great hall itself has become the focal point of a major renewal that attracts countless visitors to lively attractions and a new sense of history that mingles old and new.

Opposite: *An exterior view of this landmark in American agriculture, with its upper-story clerestory and rooftop cupola, preserved as a working farm-museum at Hancock Shaker Village.*

> *"Do all your work as though you had a thousand years to live on earth, as you would if you knew you must die tomorrow"*
>
> —Shaker Mother Ann Lee

IN THE ROUND

The Shaker sect, an offshoot of the Quakers, emigrated from England in 1774 under the leadership of Mother Ann Lee, whom they recognized as the inspired head of the Church of God on earth. They called themselves the United Society of Believers, but became known as the Shakers (or Shaking Quakers) because of the fervor of their liturgical dancing and chanting. They formed celibate communities in which the men and women lived in separate quarters and came together for communal labor, primarily farming, craftsmanship, and the preparation of herbal remedies for sale to neighboring farms and towns, which held them in high respect.

The round barn at Hancock Shaker Village is an enduring tribute to the Shaker masons and carpenters who constructed it on the stone foundations of an earlier barn built during the 1820s. The structure is 90 feet in diameter with fieldstone walls almost a yard thick. The band of windows in the second-story clerestory, and the multipaned windows in the main structure, admit healthful light, while the cupola serves as a ventilator.

The hay mow measures 55 feet across and is separated from the wide, circular feeding aisle by a low parapet, behind which stalls for fifty-two dairy cows provided ample accommodation for a very large herd, which could be attended to with much less labor than the average rectangular barn required.

Both round and polygonal barns had been recommended to farmers a decade earlier by phrenologist Orson S. Fowler, who had been a zealous promoter of octagonal houses since 1845 in his book *A Home for All.* In 1853 he asserted that "In [barns] especially we need some common center in and around which to work. This form will turn heads of the horses and cattle, and openings

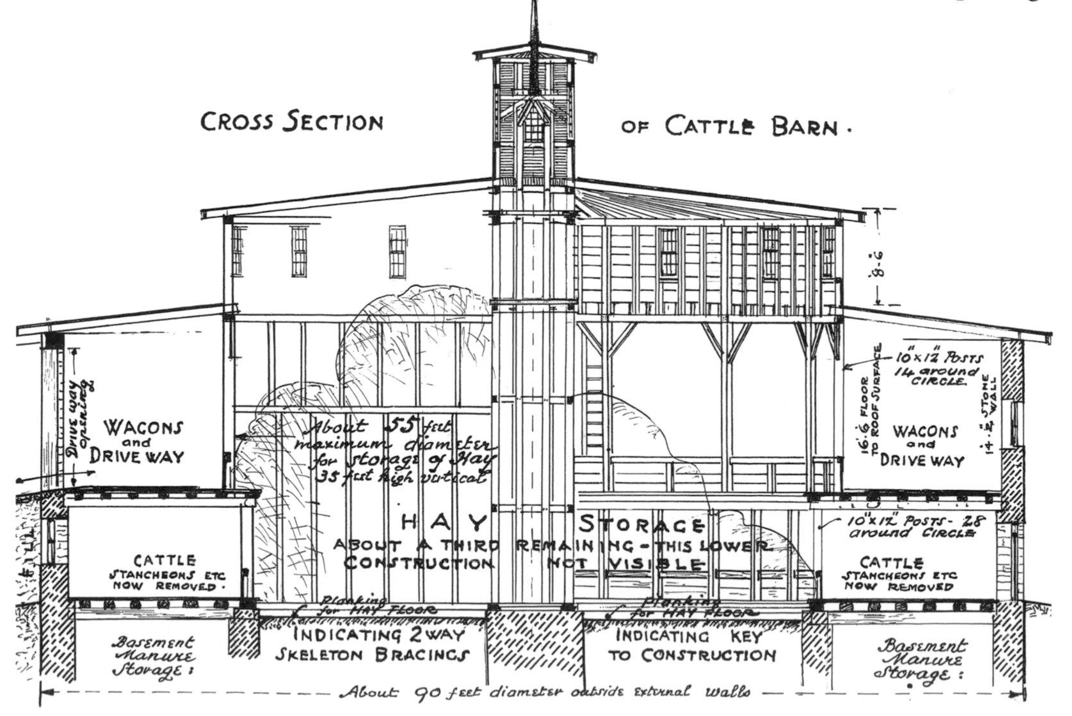

Right: *A cross section of the remarkable circular masonry barn built by the Shaker community of Hancock, Massachusetts, in 1865.*

Overleaf: *Strong timber framing forms an octagonal pillar in the center of the barn that soars toward the multiraftered ceiling to support the superstructure. A plan of the building is shown on the facing page.*

> *"Went to see the Round Stone Barn; it is a very curious and singular constructed building..."*
>
> —Sister Lucy Hammond

to all the bays and bins, toward the center." We have no way of ascertaining whether the industrious Shakers were influenced by Fowler's ideas, but many progressive farmers of the late nineteenth century concurred with the opinion of an influential farm journal—that the round barn at Hancock was "a model for the soundest dairying practice."

AT A GLANCE: ROUND BARN, HANCOCK SHAKER VILLAGE

- The barn was extensively rebuilt at a cost of $10,000 by Shaker masons and carpenters in 1865 after fire destroyed much of the original 1820s barn.
- The efficient circular design enables the use of minimal walling to enclose maximum interior space. Its 270-foot circumference encircles over 5,500 square feet of land.
- The clerestory-windowed second story and turret were an innovation, drawing comparisons to "a small hat box on a larger one."

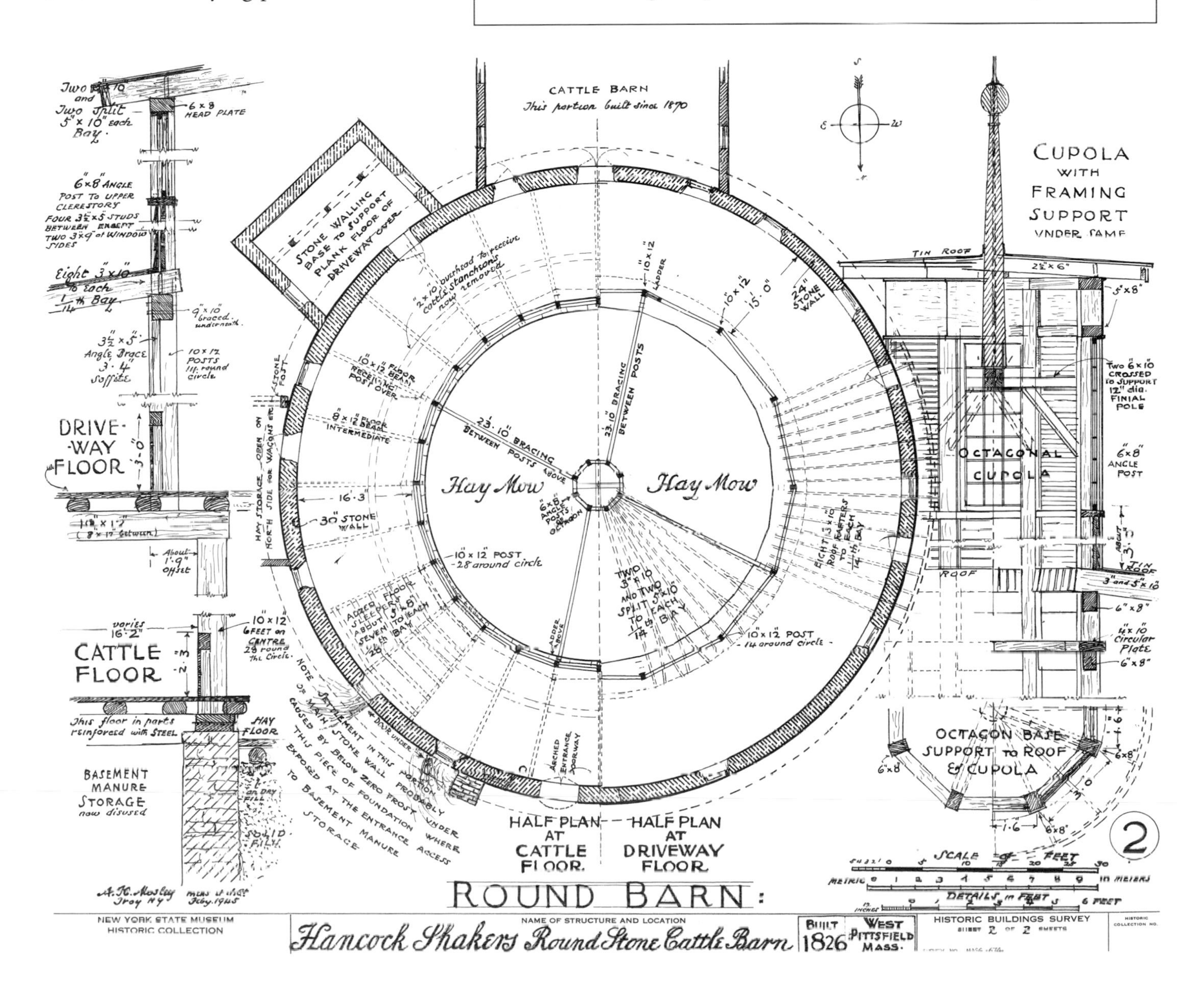

TOUCHED WITH FIRE

Like many early nineteenth-century forts, historic Fort Sumter is a pentagonal structure with walls 8 to 12 feet thick to sustain bombardment from heavy guns. Named for a great South Carolina hero of the Revolutionary War, it was designed in 1827 as part of a defensive system for the major port of Charleston and built on a man-made island of sea shells and granite from Northern quarries. Fifty feet high, it was still incomplete and without major armament in 1860, when the election of Abraham Lincoln precipitated the secession of South Carolina early in 1861. Major Robert Anderson of the U.S. Army was in charge of the garrison at Fort Sumter, which was still at work on strengthening the position. When provisional Confederate forces in Charleston, led by Brigadier General Beauregard, demanded the surrender of Fort Sumter, and Anderson refused, the opening engagement of the Civil War took place with the bombardment of the fort on April 12–13, 1861. Major Anderson was forced to surrender and evacuated his garrison on the following day.

"If Anderson was obstinate—[my husband] was to order the forts on our side to open fire. Certainly fire had begun. The regular roar of the cannon—there it was. And who could tell what each volley accomplished of death and destruction."

—from the journal entry of a Charleston resident, April 12, 1861.

AT A GLANCE: FORT SUMTER

- Named in honor of the last surviving officer of the Revolutionary War, Brigadier General, Congressman, and U.S. Senator Thomas Sumter (1734–1832), the fort at the mouth of Charleston Harbor is the site of the Civil War's first battle.
- Under the command of Major Robert Anderson, with a force of fewer than 100 Federal troops and armed with only 48 of the 140 cannon that it was designed to mount, the fort was besieged by Confederate forces for 34 hours on April 12-13, 1861.
- The fort suffered heavy damage but no casualties, and Anderson surrendered due to lack of resources and certainty of defeat. Four years later, at the end of the war, he returned to raise the American flag that had flown over his garrison.

"Great Balls of Fire!"
—Otis Blackwell

A LONG SHOT

This unusual structure, built 1828–29, is one of a very few examples of the shot towers once used to make ammunition by dropping molten lead from the top of the tower through a sievelike device into a vat of cold water below. The lead formed balls as it fell, and the water caught and cooled the shot. It was then hardened, hand-dried, and sorted into 25-pound bags.

AT A GLANCE: PHOENIX SHOT TOWER

- The tower's cornerstone was laid in 1828 by Charles Carroll, the last surviving signatory to the Declaration of Independence.
- At 234 feet, the tower was the nation's tallest until the erection of the Washington Monument. Its diameter is 40 feet at the base and 20 at the top. The walls are 4.5 feet thick at the base, 20 inches thick at the top, and contain more than one million bricks.
- Shot was manufactured by the hoisting of molten lead to "dropping stations," where it was passed through a perforated pan. The lead droplets formed perfect spheres as they plunged toward a cooling cistern of water at the tower's base.

Built by the Phoenix Shot Tower Company of Baltimore, Maryland, this tower, which comprises more than a million bricks, was constructed without the use of scaffolding. It tapers from a wall thickness of 4.5 feet at street level to only 20 inches diameter at the apex. Its cornerstone was laid by Charles Carroll of Carrolton, one of the signers of the Declaration of Independence. It stands at the corner of Fallsway and Fayette Streets in Baltimore, and was once the tallest structure in the United States, until completion of the Washington Monument. The tower and its adjacent plant were acquired by the Merchant's Shot Tower Company, who continued to manufacture ammunition here until 1894.

Union Oil bought the facility in 1921 with the intention of tearing it down and building a gas station in its place, but civic outcry saved the tower, which Union Oil then gave to the city. It was restored in 1976 and opened to the public as a museum for some time. At this writing, the Shot Tower Museum is under renovation and is scheduled to reopen to the public in 2002.

"A drowsy, dreamy influence seems to hang over the land, and to pervade the very atmosphere."

—Washington Irving,
The Legend of Sleepy Hollow

***Right:** An aerial view of the nation's best-known estate in the Gothic Revival style.*

AMERICAN GOTHIC

Architect Alexander Jackson Davis, master of many Victorian-era styles, surpassed himself with his design for this masonry residence in New York's Hudson Valley. Built in 1842 as a country residence for then-mayor of New York City William Paulding, this was Davis's second full-fledged essay in the Gothic Revival style: the first was Glen Ellen, built in Baltimore, Maryland, in 1832. Glen Ellen, too, was inspired by the picturesque and imposing style introduced in England during the mid-eighteenth century by Sir Horace Walpole, who remodeled his country estate in the medieval mode, recalling its battlements, roof pinnacles, turrets, pointed-arch windows, and decorative stone tracery. However, the style did not gain currency in the United States for almost a century. In fact, Lyndhurst (or Knoll, as he called it), was initially referred to as "Paulding's Folly" by critics of its Romantic asymmetrical appearance.

However, tastes were changing rapidly in a time of major social change and burgeoning wealth, and within a few decades wealthy New Yorkers became enamored of the Romanticism that had come to dominate the arts, including architecture, especially in the Hudson River Valley. Lyndhurst's second owner, George Merritt, commissioned Davis to double the size of the

***Right:** Front elevation (facing the river) of Lyndhurst as enlarged for its second owner, George Merritt, in 1867.*

estate. The cohesive additions were made in the same materials—brick overlaid with marble from nearby Ossining, New York—with bay windows and balconies of masterful detailing.

The house's third owner was the railroad tycoon Jay Gould, who purchased it in 1880 as a country retreat. Its parklike grounds included rolling lawns dotted with elegant specimen trees and shrubs and a curving entrance drive from which the natural setting unfolded in the fashionable "surprise views" of the period. Evergreen trees accentuated the angular Gothic roofline. At the height of his financial power in the late 1880s, Gould contracted tuberculosis, and he lived at Lyndhurst until his death in 1892. The house passed to his daughter, philanthropist Helen Gould Shepherd, and then to her sister Anna, who had married into the French nobility. It was Anna, Duchess of Talleyrand-Perigord, who maintained the estate until her death in 1961, when Lyndhurst became the property of the National Trust for Historic Preservation.

AT A GLANCE: LYNDHURST

- Built in 1838 by Alexander Jackson Davis for New York City Mayor William Paulding, who named it Knoll, Lyndhurst was given its present name by the second owner, merchant George Merritt, for the Linden trees planted on the estate.
- The Gothic Revival mansion, one of the nation's finest, was developed extensively over 100 years and is home to America's first steel-framed conservatory.
- The estate neighbors that of Washington Irving, author of *The Legend of Sleepy Hollow* and *Rip van Winkle.*

***Below:** This elegant landmark adorns its setting like the topmost jewel in a crown.*

AT A GLANCE: THE HERMITAGE PLANTATION

- The Hermitage Plantation House was designed and built after the Greek Revival style in 1820 by its owner Henry McAlpin, one of the South's wealthiest men.
- The plantation's industries included not only agriculture but also manufacture of rice barrels, cast iron, bricks, and lumber.
- By 1850, 60 million bricks had been produced for Savannah buildings, including, unusually, slave dwellings on the plantation itself. Henry Ford used Hermitage grey Savannah bricks for his summerhouse in Richmond Hill.

"I beg to present you as a Christmas gift the city of Savannah, with one hundred and fifty heavy guns and plenty of ammunition; also about twenty-five thousand bales of cotton."

—William T. Sherman,
to President Lincoln, 1864

GEORGIA ON MY MIND

Not to be confused with President Andrew Jackson's Tennessee home of the same name, the site of Savannah's Hermitage Plantation was acquired by the wealthy businessman Henry McAlpin in 1814. He kept the name "Hermitage," bestowed by the property's previous owner, the French Huguenot M. Montilet, but designed his own house in the Greek Revival style, completed in 1820. Built on a point overlooking the Savannah River, like so many Southern plantations, the house is constructed of stuccoed brick over a high arcaded basement and is a single story tall, although its columned verandah makes it appear higher. Twin curving stairways ascend to the portico. Unusually, the front and rear façades are identical. Part of the property, which became a brick-making center for the city of Savannah as well as an agricultural enterprise, comprises "glebe lands" originally granted by King George III to the city's Christ Church, Episcopal. McAlpin founded one of the nation's earliest iron railways to link the brick kilns at his estate, using Hermitage cast iron.

The house has not been occupied since it was sacked by Union General William T. Sherman on his notorious "March to the Sea," but descendants of the slaves who had built The Hermitage continued to live in its original brick slave quarters for generations after the Civil War. Today, two of the original fifty-two slave dwellings have been re-created at Michigan's Greenfield Village.

"The world changes, we do not. Therein lies the irony that finally kills us."
—Anne Rice

ANTEBELLUM ELEGANCE

Now a National Historic Landmark, Oak Alley, a two-story Greek Revival-style mansion, was built in 1837–39 by Jacques Roman, a wealthy French sugar planter, for his new bride. Long a region of French settlement, Louisiana's "River Road" along the Mississippi, from New Orleans north to St. Francisville, was lined with such plantations, surrounded by vast green fields of sugar cane. More than half of the nation's millionaires lived in this valley during the 1850s, before the Civil War brought vast changes to their former way of life.

AT A GLANCE: OAK ALLEY

- When Oak Alley was originally constructed, between 1837 and 1839, it was known as *Bon Sejour.*
- The mansion's twenty-eight Tuscan columns are a tribute to the twenty-eight oaks forming the avenue.
- Heavy 16-inch-thick walls and a 13-foot shady veranda help cool the house during the hot Louisiana summers.
- Evidence of supernatural phenomena that are reported to have occurred at Oak Alley include sudden changes in temperature and photographic images that appear to show ghostly apparitions.
- The estate's movie credits include *Interview with the Vampire* (Warner Brothers, 1994) and *Primary Colors* (Universal, 1998).

AT A GLANCE: LOWELL TEXTILE MILLS

- Entrepreneurs acquired a site for textile production next to the Merrimack River in 1821. Development followed rapidly, and the new settlement, named for industrialist Frances Cabot Lowell, became the second-largest city in New England within two decades.

- The Boott Cotton Mill, first constructed in 1835, is one of the nation's oldest surviving textile mills and contains eighty-eight fully operative power looms. Commercial production ceased in 1957, but the mill and looms have been preserved as a reconstruction of 1920s textile processing techniques.

"The very river that moves the machinery in the mill...seems to acquire a new character from the fresh buildings of bright red brick and painted wood among which it takes its course; and to be as light-headed, thoughtless, and brisk a young river, in its murmurings and tumblings, as one would desire to see."

—Charles Dickens

Below: *the southwest elevation of Mill #7, showing the power house and elevator shaft.*

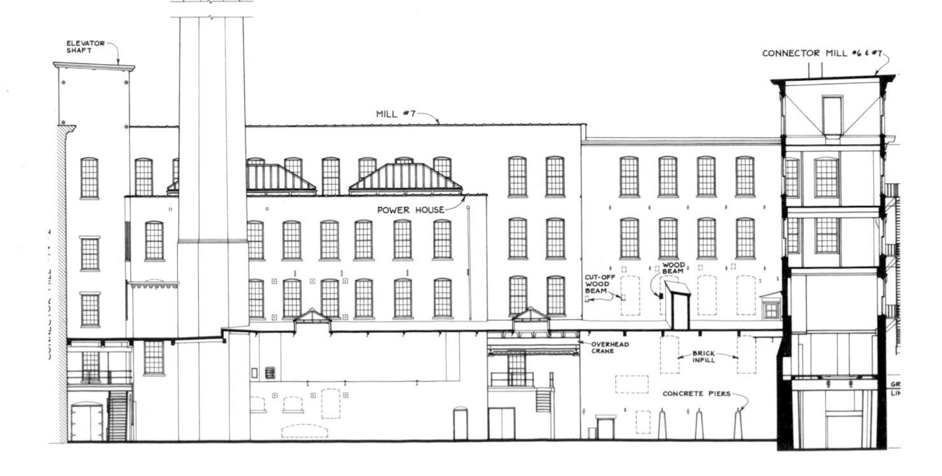

THREADS OF HISTORY

Pioneering textile manufacturer Francis Cabot Lowell (1775–1817) was born in Newburyport, Massachusetts, and first worked in the import-export trade. England's burgeoning Industrial Revolution drew him to Lancashire, where he observed newly developed textile machinery at work in the cotton mills in 1810. Upon his return, he designed from memory spinning and weaving machinery superior to the best English models with the help of Paul Moody.

"A city springing up like the enchanted palaces of the Arabian Tales, as it were in a single night—stretching far and wide its chaos of brick masonry."

—John Greenleaf Whittier

In association with his brother-in-law Patrick T. Jackson, Nathan Appleton, and others, Lowell established the Boston Manufacturing Company, which founded the first factory in the United States to perform all the operations involved in converting raw cotton into cloth (1814). Two years later, he succeeded in having a duty on cotton incorporated into the tariff laws, which opened the way for the use of cotton grown in the South to be converted into textiles in New England rather than Old England. The region quickly became a manufacturing center, and Lowell's liberal ideas on good living conditions for his workers were carried forward by his associates, who founded the industrial town of Lowell, Massachusetts, named for him, after his untimely death in 1817. Available water power from the nearby Merrimack River was the principal reason for choosing this historic site, established in 1821. It soon became the second-largest city in New England. In 1835 the Boott Cotton Mill (opposite) was constructed here and remained in production until 1957, when the textile industry had long since begun to migrate south in search of cheap labor. Fortunately, the brick mill, with its eighty-eight fully operative power looms, has been preserved as an exemplar of American industry over a period of more than 100 years.

AT A GLANCE: ELMSCOURT

- Overlooking the terminus of Mississippi's Natchez Trace, Elmscourt was originally a simple, square planter's house. The ornamentation was added during subsequent extensive renovation.
- The building's second owners, the A.P. Merrills, added the Mediterranean filigree and additional wings, giving a distinctive, elegant air to the house.
- A National Historic Site, Elmscourt has been host to, among other distinguished guests, President Ulysses S. Grant.

"We require from buildings, as from men, two kinds of goodness; first, doing their practical duty; then that they be graceful and pleasing in doing it."
—John Ruskin

THE CREOLE INFLUENCE

This gracious ornament to the Natchez Trace was a wedding gift in 1830 to Mr. and Mrs. Ayres P. Merrill from Mrs. Merrill's father. The couple eventually expanded the original small, square house by the addition of large wings and the delicate lacy ironwork in the Creole style, which was imported from Italy. Similarly, the interior was beautified by the addition of elegant fretwork and numerous chandeliers: Elmscourt became known as "The Mansion of a Thousand Candles." The Merrills had seven lively children, and the house was the scene of many brilliant gatherings over the years. At one point, Ayres P. Merrill was appointed ambassador to Belgium, and his daughter Jennie honed her considerable social skills in the royal courts of Europe. Later, she moved into the mansion Glenburnie, across the road from Elmscourt, where she spent the rest of her life.

"No one in Natchez is entirely certain how many of Natchez's ante-bellum houses are haunted."
—Philip Hamburger,
An American Notebook

PIECES OF EIGHT

When this ornate, octagonal mansion began to take shape just before the Civil War, neighboring Natchez, Mississippi, plantation owners called it "Nutt's Folly." It was built by Haller Nutt, whose father was an eccentric adventurer who made a fortune and set up his son as a cotton planter. Young Haller's plans were influenced by his father's interest in Moorish palaces and arabesques, and by the octagonal form of building espoused by Orson Squire Fowler, who sought to convince Americans that eight-sided buildings could enclose more space than four-sided buildings and promote more healthful living. The enthusiastic newlywed wanted to provide a unique home for his bride, Julia Williams, and engaged the eminent Philadelphia architect Samuel Sloan to draw up the blueprints. As it stands, Longwood is six stories high, surmounted by an onion-shaped dome, and surrounded by ornate galleries. The house has a profusion of narrow arched windows augmented by large mirrors in the dome and smaller ones downstairs to provide indirect lighting. Of its thirty-two rooms, only nine are finished: the outbreak of the Civil War sent construction workers scattering before Nutt's elaborate plans for furnishing the house with treasures from abroad could be carried out. Some of the furnishings had already been shipped to American warehouses and were later purchased by museums. Sadly, the owner died before the war was over, and Longwood eventually became an empty mansion/museum—the monument to a dream.

AT A GLANCE. LONGWOOD

- Designed by Philadelphia architect Samuel Sloan for the wealthy physician and plantation owner Dr. Haller Nutt, Longwood is reputedly the largest octagonal mansion in the nation.
- Timber used in the ornamental woodwork was shipped to Philadelphia where it was hand-carved and returned to Natchez in its finished state.
- Construction began around 1860, but was halted at the outbreak of the Civil War when only the basement was completed. Work was never resumed, and the building remains, with its bare-brick and empty upper floors, unfinished to this day.

AT A GLANCE: THE STAR BARN

- Built by master carpenter Daniel Reichert in 1868 in the traditional style of the Pennsylvania German/Swiss barn, the distinctive cupola, spire, and louvers bear star and lancet motifs that are definitively Gothic in style.

- The barn complex is also named for gentleman farmer, horse breeder, and financier John Motter, who made his fortune supplying livestock to the army during the Civil War and constructed the buildings to mark his success.

- A successful campaign to save the barn was launched by Friends of the Star Barn and Preservation Pennsylvania.

- The building was added to the National Register of Historic Places in 2000, and is now preserved for the nation.

"I expect to pass through this world but once. Any good therefore that I can do, or any kindness that I can show to any fellow creature, let me do it now."

—William Penn

PENNSYLVANIA DUTCH

This handsome old, weathered barn in Highspire, Pennsylvania, is typical of the "banked barns" built by German and Amish settlers. Their barns were banked into a slope for weather protection with livestock quarters below and haymows and threshing floor in the overhanging forebay. This example was built for a wealthy farmer by master carpenter Daniel Reichert. It is unusual in having a front-facing gable in the Gothic Revival style (or "Rustic Pointed"), as well as pointed louvered windows and a louvered star and cupola for ventilation.

"A sea of sin, lashed by the tempest of lust and passion."
—Reverend F.M. Warrington

ALL THAT GLITTERS

An exclamation point in California's colorful history, the mining town of Bodie was established as placer mining declined along the western slopes of the Sierra Nevada and the rush to the high desert country began. What would become one of the richest sources of gold and silver in Western history was discovered by Waterman S. Body and fellow prospector Black Taylor in 1859 (the spelling of the town's name was soon changed to Bodie to avoid mispronunciation). This may have been Bodie's most conservative decision, as the town soon became a byword for lawlessness and license of every kind, after the Standard Mining Company made an incredibly rich strike here in 1877. Gold fever spread like wildfire, and during its heyday (1879–81) Bodie had more than sixty saloons and dance halls, a thriving business in prostitution along Bonanza Street, and, by most accounts, a murder almost daily. Like many Old West towns, it featured a main street lined with false-front buildings. Rooms were available for a dollar a night, and mills churned twenty-four hours a day. However, mining diminished and businesses were abandoned long before the disastrous fire of 1932, which destroyed all but 10 percent of the town. What had become the ghost town of Bodie was designated a National Historic Site and a State Historic Park in 1962. Now tourists walk the deserted streets, where sagging wooden buildings, high winds, and perhaps the occasional ghost are all that remains of the notorious boom town.

AT A GLANCE: BODIE HISTORIC PARK

- Named for Waterman S. Body, who struck gold here in 1859, the ghost town that is now Bodie State Historic Park was once home to 2,000 buildings and 10,000 inhabitants. It boomed in 1877 when the Standard Mining Company made a huge strike of gold and silver ore.

- Fortune hunters came from far and wide, and high crime rates resulted from the wild lifestyles they adopted. The phrase "Goodbye, God, I'm going to Bodie," penned by a little girl en route to the town, became known throughout the West.

- A fire, rumored to have been started by a toddler, "Bodie Bill," playing with matches, destroyed 90 percent of the town. Its remains are preserved in a state of suspended dereliction.

"You are entitled to food, clothing, shelter and medical attention. Anything else you get is a privilege."
—Regulation 5, U.S.P. Alcatraz.

THE ROCK

This desolate, 12-acre island overlooking the entrance to San Francisco Harbor's Golden Gate has been viewed as a strategic site since California was controlled by New Spain. It was first visited and then fortified by the Spanish before it came under American control in 1849. John Fremont, acting governor of California, purchased it in the name of the United States for $5,000. By 1853 a construction detail had arrived and within the following year, an inspection report stated that "Temporary buildings for the accommodation of workmen have been erected, excavations made, and masonry commenced....The batteries on this island might be completed in about one year."

More than a mile of cold, rough water separates the island from the mainland, which led to its use as a military prison from 1859 onward, when an army post had been established here. During the Civil War, it mounted a series of encircling batteries and constructed a massive brick guardhouse and a three-story barracks that could accommodate 600 men. Political prisoners were incarcerated here during the war—a harbinger of things to come. In 1868 the post became a disciplinary barracks and military prison for, among others, Native Americans who resisted confinement to reservations. During the Spanish-American War (1900), Filipino prisoners were sent here, and conscientious objectors were interned at Alcatraz during World War I. By this time, an army report had complained that "Sanitary defects of the prison are especially apparent at this season of the year. The ventilation of the buildings is very faulty. The prisoner [who is] locked in for the night is virtually boxed in for so many hours....The means available for solitary confinement are such as have long been discarded in the better class of civilian penal establishments."

The rise of organized crime during the 1930s led the Federal Bureau of Prisons

***Right:** "Frowning Alcatraz, Key of San Francisco," described the fortress built here in 1866 to command the entrance to the Golden Gate with some of the heaviest guns ever cast to that date.*

to take over the former fortress as a maximum-security federal penitentiary (1934). The name "Alcatraz" soon became a byword for harsh treatment of prisoners, and several unsuccessful escape attempts ended in punitive treatment upon recapture, or drowning in the cold, turbulent waters of the bay. Difficulties in supplying the facility led to its closure in 1963, and in 1969 a group of Native American activists made a two-year attempt to establish a base on "The Rock." Since 1972 the notorious island has been part of the Golden Gate National Recreation Area and, ironically, a major tourist attraction.

AT A GLANCE: ALCATRAZ

- Alcatraz Island was given its name in 1775 by the Spanish explorer Juan Manuel de Ayala, who christened it *Isla de los Alcatraces*—Island of the Pelicans—for its only inhabitants.

- Alcatraz Island lies 1.25 miles offshore and was the site of the first operational lighthouse on the West Coast. Contrary to legend, only small, bottom-feeding sharks inhabit the waters and the chief hazards for escapees were chilly waters and strong currents.

- Famous inmates include gangster Al Capone; Robert Stroud, the "Birdman of Alcatraz"; and George "Machine Gun" Kelly.

Left: *"Broadway" was the nickname given to the corridor looking south between cell blocks C and B, when Alcatraz was a maximum-security federal prison for dangerous prisoners (1933–63).*

Overleaf: *A chilling view of the three-tiered isolation wing, in which prisoners considered especially dangerous or rebellious were confined in small cells without communication or privileges of any kind.*

Please do not handle doors.
Bitte, nicht die Türen anfassen.
No toque las puertas, gracias.
3B
11
12
13
11
12

"As long as the Salt Lake Temple stands, there will be a magnificent monument to the patience, skill and dedication of its architect."

— Wendell Ashton

IN SEARCH OF ZION

Unlike the countless European immigrants who came to the United States in flight from religious persecution, the founding members of the Church of Jesus Christ of Latter-day Saints, called the Mormons, were Americans who founded a religious community based on revelations to their prophet Joseph Smith by the Angel Moroni at Fayette, New York, in 1820. The original band of Saints, as they called themselves, numbered only thirty, but they were deeply committed to founding a Utopian community in which they could practice their new faith, as first written down by Smith in the Book of Mormon. They sent out missionaries into nearby areas and built their first temple in Kirtland, Ohio—an eclectic building combining Federal, Greek, and Gothic elements. Some members went on to settle in Missouri, but they were driven out and moved to Nauvoo, Illinois, where, in 1844, a mob attacked and killed Joseph Smith and his brother Hyrum. Brigham Young, designated the President of the Twelve Apostles, led the exodus from Nauvoo to the arid Great Basin, where the community founded its State of Deseret in what would become the Utah Territory.

Inspired by the indomitable Young, the Mormons prospered here through every adversity. Work on the sacred, multispired Mormon Temple at the heart of Temple Square began only six years after the hard-working community entered the Salt Lake Valley in 1853. Brigham Young conceived the design, with its ornamental

AT A GLANCE: THE MORMON TEMPLE

- The Temple's design was sketched by President Brigham Young in 1853 and passed to architect Truman O. Angell to complete. Construction was completed forty years later.
- A 13-foot-high statue of the Angel Moroni adorns one of the building's six spires.
- Only Latter-day Saints are allowed access to the interior of the sacred Mormon Temple.
- Granite used to build the structure was quarried and transported by ox and cart from Cottonwood Canyon, 20 miles away.
- The structure is 210 feet tall at its apex, the east tower, and 118 feet wide at its widest point.
- The building's walls are 8 feet thick, tapering to 6 feet as they rise skyward. They are supported by 15-foot-wide foundations.

Opposite: *The Tabernacle under construction, with the ground plan shown below.*

Below: *Temple Square, with the Tabernacle to the left of the Temple.*

celestial bodies carved into the granite, and architect Truman O. Angell spent the rest of his life carrying out the commission, which he did not live to see completed. Blocks of stone were hauled from canyons 20 miles away by teams of oxen before a railroad was constructed. Sculptor Cyrus E. Dallin created the statue of the Book of Mormon annunciant, the Angel Moroni, to crown the tallest of the Temple's six spires, on the 210-foot-tall eastern elevation. The Temple's precincts are open only to members of the Mormon faith. Here, weddings, baptisms, and "sealings" of those who were not born into the Mormon community are carried out. (The original Mormon practice of polygamy was eventually outlawed, but Brigham Young had twenty-seven wives, and most other nineteenth-century Mormons adhered to this practice to build up the church.)

"This is the right place!"
— Brigham Young

Close by the Temple is the world-famous Mormon Tabernacle, with a capacity of 8,000. It was built between 1865 and 1867, with a vaulted ceiling and roof that have been credited to engineer Henry Grow, who was a bridge builder experienced with the Remington-type truss. This curved truss is formed of pine timbers secured at joints with 2-inch wooden pegs and lashed with rawhide thongs at intermediate points. This architecturally unique American auditorium is approximately 150 feet wide and 250 feet long, with straight side walls terminating in semicircular end walls. Heavy stone piers projecting at intervals of about 14 feet act as support for the roof trusses; like the foundations, they are made of local sandstone. Originally, the roof was covered with wood shingles, which were replaced first with copper, then with aluminum. The gallery was added in 1870 to improve the acoustics of the hall. The renowned Mormon Tabernacle Choir performs here regularly, and a host of musicians, singers, and conductors from around the world have appeared on its stages and podiums since 1884. The Tabernacle's massive pipe organ, with its 11,623 pipes, dominates the interior, which also serves as a gathering place for Church conferences.

The beautiful Temple Square gardens include many plants indigenous to the region with histories and associations of their own, including the "bride's trees" near the Temple and the Grand Lawn, which helps unite Temple Square's other structures, including the Assembly Hall and two modern visitors' centers, as well as monuments to Utah's history.

AT A GLANCE: THE MORMON TABERNACLE

- According to legend, the Brigham Young-designed dome was inspired by the shape of a cracked egg.
- The Tabernacle seats 8,000 and is 250 feet long and 150 feet wide.
- Forty-four sandstone piers support the dome, which to this day contains the original Ithiel Town arch system, a lattice-truss construction consisting of pine beams held together with rawhide.
- Since its construction in 1967, additions to the structure include a gallery in 1870 to remedy acoustic problems and an aluminum roof in 1910, replacing the original wood shingle.

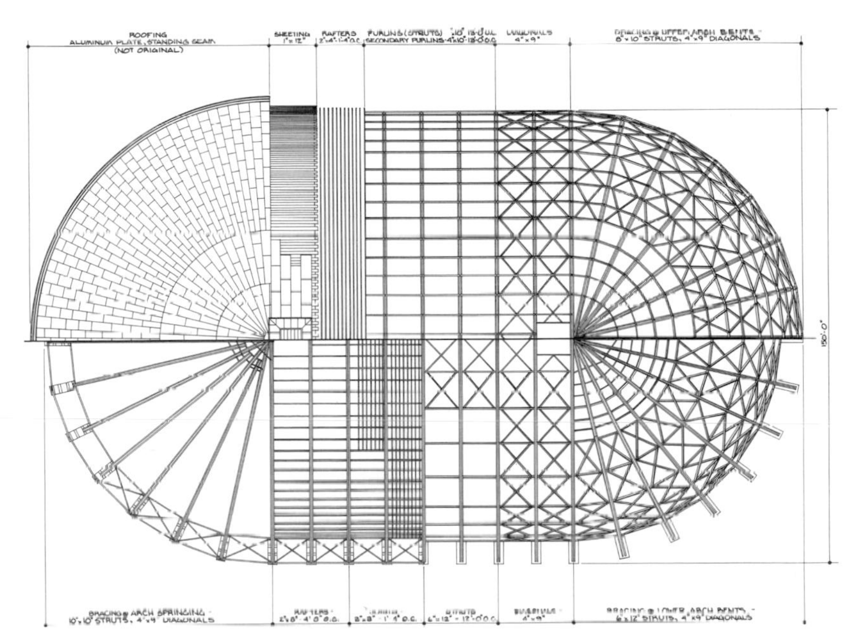

"A majestic and lovely show there in the moonlight...silent, weird, beautiful."
—Walt Whitman

CITY OF BROTHERLY LOVE

Designed by John McArthur, Jr., this is the largest and most elaborate city hall in the United States that is still in use. It is also the world's tallest bearing-wall structure laid up without steel framing. The width of its stone walls ranges from 22 feet at ground level to 6 feet at the apex. Work began on the site in 1871, and the first foundation stone was laid the following year. Funding issues caused many of the delays that resulted in legislators waiting until 1901 for their offices to be ready.

The opulent French Second Empire style of the building, with its numerous carved sculptures by Alexander Milne Calder and assistants, drew both praise and criticism during its long period of construction. The inner courtyard resembles that of a French chateau of the Renaissance Revival era, and many of the public rooms are vast and inspiring, notably the Mayor's Reception Room and the City Council Chamber, which are especially rich in sculptural ornamentation.

The tower view is City Hall's proudest boast and is accessible by escalators and elevator. The 37-foot bronze statue of William Penn by Calder, recently restored, is one of Philadelphia's best-loved landmarks, and the view from the top of the building encompasses the whole city and its suburbs, as well as the upper and lower Delaware Valley and port and western New Jersey. Acclaimed works by A.M. Calder's descendants are also visible from this height. Sculptures by Alexander Sterling Calder (1871–1945) and Alexander Calder (1898–1976) adorn Logan Circle and the Philadelphia Museum of Art.

AT A GLANCE: PHILADELPHIA CITY HALL

- Three decades passed between the groundbreaking and dedication of the nation's most awe-inspiring example of French Second Empire architecture, during which such technological breakthroughs as electricity forced many changes to the plans, including replacing the originally specified gas lamps.

- Occupying 4.5 acres of land and 700 rooms, the building cost more than $24 million. The huge cost of demolition and replacement kept it safe from destruction before National Landmark status was granted.

- More than 500 feet tall, the tower is one of the tallest masonry structures in the world. A vast statue of William Penn, with 30-inch fingers and an 18-inch nose, stands atop the building.

"Rare felicity of the times when it is permitted to think what you like and say what you think."
—Tacitus; rotunda inscription

STATE OF GOOD HOPE

This elegant state capitol (1892–1905) is a synthesis of ancient and modern Classical elements. Its high central dome crowns a rotunda whose symmetrical second-story stairways lead to the House and Senate chambers. A mural in the rotunda depicts the first settlement of Providence by dissenters from the Puritan regime of the Massachusetts Bay Colony. As Robert A.M. Stern observes in *Pride of Place* (Houghton Mifflin, 1986): "Rhode Island, the smallest yet one of the richest states, memorialized its role as one of the founding thirteen [colonies] by building a grandly Roman marble palace that brought to scholarly perfection the forms that had evolved in Washington for over seventy years."

AT A GLANCE: RHODE ISLAND STATE HOUSE

- The Rhode Island State House has the largest freestanding marble dome in the nation and the second largest in the world, with a diameter of 50 feet and a depth, from its square base to its apex, of 149 feet.
- Charles Follen McKim's design cost over $3 million to construct, and used vast quantities of materials: 15 million bricks, 327,000 cubic feet of Georgia marble, and more than 1,000 tons of iron floor beams.
- Rhode Island has the longest official name of any state—State of Rhode Island and Providence Plantations.
- The statue of the Independent Man atop the State House dome symbolizes the state's history as a haven for religious dissenters.
- The rotunda features a mural depicting Roger Williams and his fellow dissenters founding Providence.

"And o'er them the lighthouse looked lovely as hope."
—Paul Moon James, The Beacon.

BEACON OF HOPE

This imposing conical lighthouse—the tallest on the continent at 208 feet—was first built in 1802 to warn mariners away from the treacherous Diamond Shoals, whose shallow, offshore reefs, subject to unpredictable currents, claimed hundreds of ships before the light was erected. It was mandated by Henry Dearborn, a Revolutionary War veteran and congressman, and stood 95 feet above sea level. Then the United States Lighthouse Board intervened in 1853 and had the coastal Cape Hatteras Light raised to a height of 150 feet and equipped with a first-order Fresnel lens—the most powerful devised by nineteenth-century technology, in the person of the French inventor Augustin-Jean Fresnel.

Right: *The beam from the tallest lighthouse in North America can be seen many miles offshore.*

AT A GLANCE:
CAPE HATTERAS LIGHTHOUSE

- There has been a light at Cape Hatteras since 1802, warning mariners of North Carolina's hazardous Diamond Shoals, offshore shallow reefs with unpredictable currents. High seas, caused by tempestuous conditions and the collision of the warm Gulf Stream and cooler Virginia Coastal Current, have claimed more than 600 ships here; hence the area's nickname "The Graveyard of the Atlantic."

- The present structure was erected in 1870 and, at 208 feet, is the nation's tallest lighthouse. It weighs 6,250 tons and was built with 1.25 million bricks baked in kilns along Virginia's James River and transported by barge to the Outer Banks.

- The lighthouse was moved in 1999 as coastal erosion, caused by the Atlantic waves, threatened to undermine its foundations.

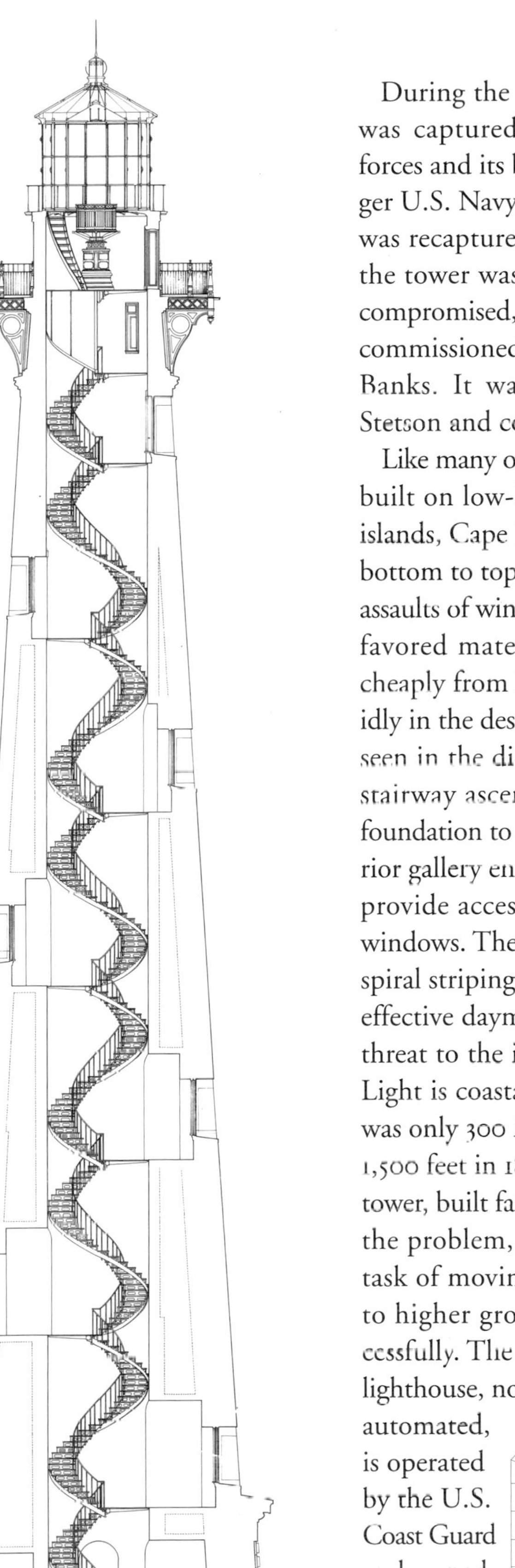

During the Civil War, the lighthouse was captured briefly by Confederate forces and its beacon removed to endanger U.S. Navy warships. When the light was recaptured and restored to service, the tower was found to be structurally compromised, and still another light was commissioned at Buxton, on the Outer Banks. It was engineered by Dexter Stetson and constructed in 1870.

Like many of the traditional lighthouses built on low-lying beaches and barrier islands, Cape Hatteras was tapered from bottom to top to make it resistant to the assaults of wind and waves. Brick was the favored material, as it could be made cheaply from local clay and laid up rapidly in the desired number of courses. As seen in the diagram at left, a spiral iron stairway ascends from the rubblestone foundation to the lantern room. An exterior gallery encircles the lantern room to provide access for cleaning its exterior windows. The dramatic black-and-white spiral striping of the walls makes this an effective daymark as well. The principal threat to the integrity of Cape Hatteras Light is coastal erosion. By the 1930s, it was only 300 feet from the ocean, versus 1,500 feet in 1802. A temporary skeleton tower, built farther inland, failed to solve the problem, and in 1999, the epochal task of moving the 6,250-ton structure to higher ground was carried out successfully. The lighthouse, now automated, is operated by the U.S. Coast Guard and owned by the National Park Service.

Overleaf: *The dramatic spiral black-and-white pattern makes this tower an effective daymark.*

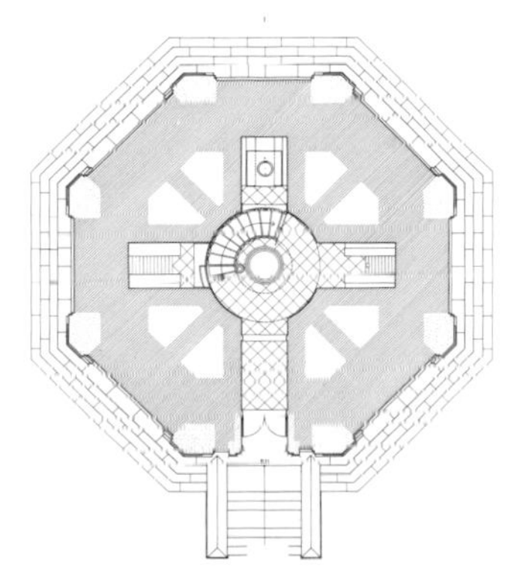

Left and below: *Sectional diagrams showing the tapered brick tower on its polygonal foundations structure.*

AT A GLANCE: MARK TWAIN HOUSE

- The Mark Twain House was designed in 1873 by architect Edward Tucker Potter with the assistance of Alfred H. Thorp, one of the first Americans to attend the prestigious *École des Beaux Arts* in Paris.

- Construction costs exceeded the family's funds and the interiors remained incomplete when they moved into the house in October 1874.

- The success of *The Adventures of Tom Sawyer*, published in 1876, followed by a series of lecture tours, enabled Clemens to enlarge the house and commission Louis Comfort Tiffany's firm, Associated Artists, to decorate its first floor.

"To us, our house…had a heart, and a soul…it was of us, and we were in its confidence and lived in its grace and in the peace of its benediction. We never came from an absence that its face did not light up and speak out its eloquent welcome—and we could not enter unmoved."

—Mark Twain

HEART AND SOUL

The nation's best-known humorist, born Samuel Langhorne Clemens in 1835, spent some of his early years working as a Mississippi River steamboat pilot, and this is expressed in the unusual and opulent style of this house, which is often described as Steamboat Gothic. Like most writers, his fortunes waxed and waned in an erratic fashion, and after commissioning this eighteen-room mansion in the Hartford, Connecticut, literary community of Nook Farm, he had to wait some years before furnishing it in the style that he and his wife Olivia had imagined when they sketched a layout for their architect, based on views over what was then open countryside and a bend (nook) in the Park River. A series of lecture tours and the phenomenal literary success of *The Adventures of Tom Sawyer* enabled the Twains to engage Louis Comfort Tiffany's distinguished design firm, Associated Artists, to decorate the house's first floor (they also enlarged the servants' wing). The results were so pleasing that Twain wrote in 1896 to praise "the perfect taste of this ground floor, with its delicious dream of harmonious color, and its all-pervading spirit of peace and serenity and deep contentment." The house is now a National Historic Landmark.

> *"Many of the readers of* The Times *...will agree with us in the opinion that it is one of the oddest looking buildings in the State ever designed for a dwelling, if not in the whole country."*
>
> —The Hartford Daily Times, March 23, 1874

Opposite and below: *The "Steamboat Gothic" house at 351 Farmington Avenue, Hartford, Connecticut, with an interior view of the conservatory shown below.*

Right: *Boston's Copley Square, in the Back Bay area, features Trinity Church, home to a parish founded before the American Revolution.*

AT A GLANCE: TRINITY CHURCH, BOSTON

- The design of Trinity Church is derived from European architecture; the Romanesque style was founded in eleventh-century France and reinterpreted here by Henry Hobson Richardson. The central tower was modeled on that of the Old Cathedral in Salamanca, Spain.

- The church contains some of America's finest examples of devotional stained glass by such masters as John LaFarge and England's renowned Pre-Raphaelites William Morris and Sir Edward Burne-Jones.

- Four giant granite pyramids support the four pier towers, and a series of 4,500 wooden pilings ensure the structure's stability; the building is sited on reclaimed wetlands. Two thousand pilings support the 19-million-pound Lantern Tower.

"The hard, straight, unrelenting lines one is used to in other cities, gives way, in Boston, to graceful curves that go sweeping in and out in a pleasant and undulating way that impels a man to assume a luxurious waltz-step."

—Mark Twain

RICHARDSONIAN ROMANESQUE

The primary building materials of this outstanding structure (built 1872–77) are yellowish-gray Milford granite laid up in quarry-faced random ashlar (cut stone) and trimmed in Longmeadow brownstone. The octagonal church roof, and that of the 211-foot Lantern Tower, are covered with multicolored and -textured materials including slate, semiglazed red tile, and terracotta crockets (ornamental devices).

"Non sub nomine, sed sub deo et lege [Not under man, but under God and Law]."
—Inscription, Harvard Law School

UNDER GOD AND LAW

The massive arched entryways of the façade, supported on short, strong pillars grouped on single bases, mark this distinguished academic structure as Richardsonian Romanesque, as does the powerful rusticated-stone tower on the right, with its narrow arched window. Austin Hall, located at 1563 Massachusetts Avenue in Cambridge, Massachusetts, is one of the oldest buildings in the nation continuously used as a school of law. Harvard University itself was established as early as 1636 by the Massachusetts Bay Colony and named for its first benefactor, the minister John Harvard, who left his library and half his estate to what is now America's oldest university in 1638.

The building's first floor houses three large classrooms whose walls are lined with the portraits of historic English judges—part of the Law School's unique art collection. The spacious second floor was originally designed to house the law library, which was moved to Langdell Hall in 1906. It is now the Ames Courtroom, where second- and third-year students argue moot court cases before panels of practicing judges. The Criminal Justice Institute, on the building's third floor, shares space with a small courtroom and several student organizations. A major renovation of this landmark academic building was completed in 1985 with careful attention to preserving the integrity of Richardson's original design. Austin Hall is an ornament to this historic, world-renowned, and ever-growing institution of higher learning.

AT A GLANCE: AUSTIN HALL, HARVARD UNIVERSITY

- Gifted by the Boston merchant Edwin Austin in memory of his older brother Samuel, Austin Hall was built between 1881 and 1884 at a cost of $135,000.
- Henry Hobson Richardson, Harvard alumnus and *École des Beaux Arts* graduate, designed the building in his characteristic Romanesque style.
- The building is home to the world-famous Harvard Law School and the site of the distinguished Ames moot court competition, a debating contest often presided over by Supreme Court justices.

AT A GLANCE: BROOKLYN BRIDGE

- John Augustus Roebling, the bridge's architect, pioneered the use of wire rope, essential for the suspension bridge construction. The four great cables supporting the Brooklyn Bridge contain enough wire to reach from New York to London.

- Work began in January 1870, seven months after Roebling's death from tetanus, contracted on the bridge's site. His son Washington succeeded him and supervised the bridge's construction through to its completion in 1883.

- Pressurized caissons, or watertight chambers, were used to drill into the riverbed. Washington Roebling was one of many struck down by "caisson disease," or decompression sickness, and he was forced to supervise construction from his apartment.

"From Brooklyn, over the Brooklyn
Bridge, on this fine morning,
please come flying...
to the rapid rolling of thousands of
small blue drums descending out
of the mackerel sky over the glittering
grandstand of harbor-water,
please come flying."

—Elizabeth Bishop,
Invitation to Miss Marianne Moore

BRIDGE OF SIGHS

The history-making Brooklyn Bridge spans New York City's East River, uniting the boroughs of Manhattan and Brooklyn. The world's first steel-wire suspension bridge, it was thirteen years in the building and cost more than $16 mil-

Left and opposite: *Two views of the bridge and its environs, including at left, the lower Manhattan skyline in 1978, almost a quarter century prior to the destruction of the Twin Towers on September 11, 2001.*

lion. Its twin Gothic towers rise 276 feet, and when it was completed in 1883, it was the world's longest suspension bridge, as well as New York's second-tallest structure (surpassed only by the spire of Trinity Church at Broadway and Wall Street).

Brooklyn Bridge was designed by the Prussian-born American engineer and creative genius John A. Roebling, who specified that its four main cables of steel wire would be more than 15 inches thick, composed of 5,434 wires each to extend more than 3,500 feet. In the course of surveying the bridge, Roebling contracted the tetanus that proved fatal before construction began. (At least twenty other lives were claimed by accidents during construction of the bridge.)

Roebling's son, Colonel Washington Roebling, assumed the role of Chief Construction Engineer, and utilized the pressurized caissons (watertight chambers) that had been employed for bridge and lighthouse construction for some time to sink piers for the massive granite towers into the riverbed. In the process, he contracted the decompression sickness then known as caisson disease (now called "the bends") and was disabled, although he continued to supervise construction from his Brooklyn Heights home with the help of binoculars. As Colonel Roebling recalled later: "Here I was at the age of thirty-two suddenly put in charge of the most stupendous engineering project of the age!"

The deck of the Brooklyn Bridge arcs more than 1,500 feet between the Gothic towers, with side spans 930 feet each reaching from tower to shore. Hailed as the eighth wonder of the world when it opened on May 24, 1883, the Brooklyn Bridge sustained still another tragedy a week later, when pedestrians on its promenade thought the span was collapsing and panicked: twelve people were trampled in the rush to escape.

For more than a hundred years, this New York City landmark has inspired painters including Joseph Stella and such notable writers as Walt Whitman, Hart Crane, and Thomas Wolfe. (More prosaically, it soon became a household word for chicanery, when sophisticated city con men offered it for sale to unsuspecting and gullible visitors!)

AT A GLANCE: STATUE OF LIBERTY

- The Statue of Liberty, a functioning lighthouse, is among the world's most famous landmarks.
- Sculpted by August Bartholdi and engineered by Gustave Eiffel, the structure was designed, built, and assembled in Paris, then disassembled, shipped, and re-erected in New York.
- A national lottery in France raised funds for the sculpture, while Joseph Pulitzer helped to raise funds in the U.S.

***Opposite:** Constructed of some 300 copper sheets riveted to an iron-and-steel armature, the statue has a green patina caused by oxidation. Architects Richard S. Hayden and Thierry W. Despont carried out an extensive renovation in 1984–86. The beloved landmark was rededicated in 1986 and figured prominently in the Millennial Celebration of January 1, 2000.*

*"Give me your tired, your poor,
Your huddled masses yearning
to breathe free"*
—Emma Lazarus

ENLIGHTENING THE WORLD

The French historian Edouard-Rene Lefebvre de Laboulaye is credited with the inspiration for this monumental sculpture designed to symbolize the union of France and the United States in the common quest for freedom. Designed and engineered in Paris, the 151-foot-tall sculpture was re-erected in New York Harbor on Bedloe's Island (now Liberty Island) and dedicated on October 18, 1886. American architect Richard Morris Hunt designed the 154-foot-high pedestal of Stony Creek granite and concrete. This inspiring monument was the first sight of the New World for millions of immigrants who came through Ellis Island between 1892 and 1954.

The monument's symbolic elements include the broken shackles at Liberty's feet, the 21-foot torch representing the light of truth and justice, and the rayed crown, an emblem of the sun. The interior of the crown has a capacity of thirty people. The tablet in the sculpture's left hand bears the Latin inscription for "July 4, 1776."

Right and below: *The tower photograph (1960) and drawing of the west elevation of the mansion were both commissioned by the Historic American Buildings Survey.*

GREEN GABLES

As Gwyn Headley, the author of *Architectural Follies in America* (John Wiley, 1996), describes it: "This is an explosion of carpentry, a fountain of gables, turrets, windows, and balconies, a veritable wooden wonder.... More than one hundred carpenters worked on the house for two years, beginning in 1884, and when it was completed [Carson] went on to use the same architects, Samuel and Joseph Newsom of

San Francisco, to build a pretty little pink palace across the street as a wedding present for his son. The Carson House stands prominently at the top of Second Street, dominating the downtown, as assertive a piece of architecture as you will ever see. It is said to be the most photographed Victorian house in America." And it seems appropriate that California's state motto, inspired by the gold rush, gave its name to the town of Eureka ("I have found it"!). Reportedly, every kind of wood on the world market was used to create the incred-

> *"The spirit of the age is reflected in the beauty, diversity and, often, playfulness of Victorian homes."*
> —Spencer Hart

AT A GLANCE: THE CARSON HOUSE

- Designed by architect Samuel Newsom for the lumber magnate William Carson, the house was built in 1884-86 as a project to employ Carson's redwood-mill workers during a slack period. It took 100 laborers two years to build their employer's mansion.
- The building's façade ornamentation, steep intersecting gables, large verandah, and angularity make this an interesting blend of the Stick Style and the Queen Anne.

ibly detailed ornamentation that makes the house unique: it was imported by the lumber baron's ships from around the globe. Skilled carpenters undoubtedly used the popular pattern books published by the Newsom brothers to create the appliqué work, finials, bargeboards, balustrades, stickwork, and moldings seen here. (They brought out no fewer than ten such books between 1884 and 1890, from each of which full working drawings and specifications could be ordered. In fact, their *Picturesque California Homes* gave plans and elevations for a single-level Queen Anne cottage that became a forerunner of the immensely popular twentieth-century bungalow style.)

It is fun to imagine what growing up in the eighteen-room Carson House might have been like, with innumerable nooks, tower rooms, cupolas, and attic rooms to explore. Inside and out, this colorful experiment in opulence has the qualities of a fairy-tale castle.

AT A GLANCE: HOTEL DEL CORONADO

- One of the earliest and most illustrious luxury resort complexes, The Hotel Del Coronado was the first hotel and the largest building outside of New York City to use electric lighting, installed under the supervision of Thomas Edison himself.
- The hotel's distinctive roof is said to have inspired Frank L. Baum's vision for the Emerald City—the *Wizard of Oz* author was a frequent visitor and wrote a number of his *Oz* books at the hotel.
- The hotel's register reads like a copy of *Who's Who*, and includes every U.S. president since Lyndon B. Johnson. Charles Lindbergh dined at the hotel after his historic flight, and Billy Wilder's 1959 classic *Some Like it Hot*, starring Marilyn Monroe, was set here.

"The saddest thing I can imagine is to get used to luxury."
—Charlie Chaplin

***Right:** A combined cross-section and elevation drawing of "the Del's" ballroom, seen with the pool area in the photograph opposite.*

SOME LIKE IT HOT

This luxurious complex in Coronado, San Diego County, California, was designed by the Canadian architects James and Merrit Reid, who were brothers. As a result of their work as draftsmen for the Evansville & Terre Haute Railroad of Indiana, where hotel developer E.S. Babcock had been an officer, they were invited to California to design the Hotel Del Coronado in 1887. Their mandate was to "build a house that people will like to come to long after we are gone."

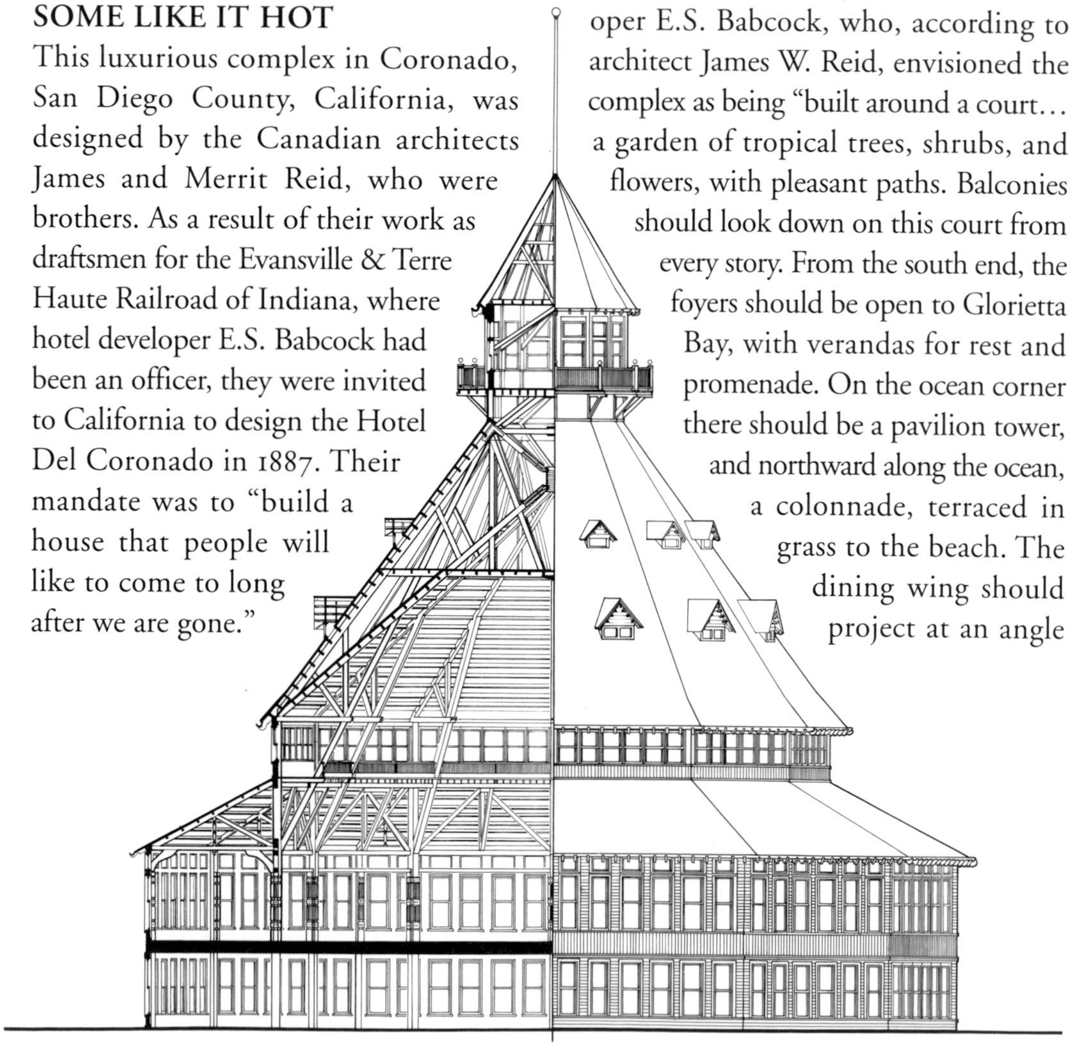

The result was this highly unusual and impressive building, which measures 250 by 440 feet and is laid out around a massive central courtyard garden. The rectangular design has four stories on the southwest elevation and five on all others, with projections at the southern and eastern corners. Wooden framing of Oregon pine on a concrete foundation remains sturdy to this day, and the multi-gabled pavilion tower (right) designed as a ballroom is among the hotel's most memorable features.

The overall plan originated with developer E.S. Babcock, who, according to architect James W. Reid, envisioned the complex as being "built around a court… a garden of tropical trees, shrubs, and flowers, with pleasant paths. Balconies should look down on this court from every story. From the south end, the foyers should be open to Glorietta Bay, with verandas for rest and promenade. On the ocean corner there should be a pavilion tower, and northward along the ocean, a colonnade, terraced in grass to the beach. The dining wing should project at an angle from the southeast corner and be almost detached, to give full value to the view of the ocean, bay, and city."

Since its grand opening in February 1888, "the Del," as it is familiarly known, has seen a steady flow of dignitaries and celebrities. In 1920 a grand banquet honoring the visiting Prince of Wales was held in the Crown Room: at this event, the prince met Mrs. Wallis Simpson, for whom he would relinquish his throne. Other notable guests include U.S. presidents Benjamin Harrison, William Howard Taft, Woodrow Wilson, Franklin D. Roosevelt, and every contemporary chief executive since Lyndon B. Johnson.

AT A GLANCE: OLANA

- Situated atop a summit in grounds designed by leading landscaper Frederick Law Olmsted (U.S. Capitol, Central Park, Biltmore Estate), "Olana" is Arabic for "our place on high." Painter Frederic Church designed the house, with the assistance of Calvert Vaux, who was responsible for structural details.
- The Moorish influence on Olana was inspired by Church's tours of the Near East and Europe.
- The Church family lived on the estate until the death of Church's son's widow in 1964. The State of New York bought the property and opened it to the public in 1967.

"I can say, as the good woman did about her mock turtle soup, 'I made it out of my own head.'"
—Frederic Church

OUR PLACE ON HIGH

Perhaps the best-known American example of the Exotic style is the Hudson River Valley estate Olana, designed by landscape painter Frederick E. Church beginning in the 1870s with the help of the fashionable architect Calvert Vaux, who had worked with landscape designer Frederick Law Olmsted on the design of New York City's Central Park. Church's dream "personal Persian" house was realized in Olana, with its multilevel roofline, Near Eastern towers, elegant archways, and Moorish detailing, commanding a site on the upper Hudson River Valley south of Albany.

The thirty-seven-room mansion, constructed of stone and wood, has an irregular layout with a full complement of towers, porches, and gazebos decorated in polychromatic style with tiles and painted brickwork. The façade openings include elegant doors and windows framed with geometric tile inlays and shaped as ogee arches—an arch of two curves meeting at a point, as in the Moorish style. The studio wing was added to the right side of the house in 1888–89, under Church's direction. He continued to make alterations to Olana until his death in 1900 and to acquire Near Eastern art and artifacts to enrich its interior.

"Irvington is the kind of village, that when you sneeze, 50 people will say 'Bless You.'"

—New York Times

AT A GLANCE: ARMOUR-STINER HOUSE

- A unique blend of Stick, Second Empire, Gothic, and Eastlake architectural styles, the Armour-Stiner House was built 1859–60.
- The rage for octagonal houses began after the publication of *A Home for All,* penned by amateur architect Orson Squire Fowler, who lauded the benefits of octagonal buildings.
- The house is named for its first two owners: Paul Armour, a financier; and Joseph Stiner, a tea importer.

ONE OF A KIND

The staid little village of Irvington, New York, must have been astonished to watch the progress of this unique octagonal house as it rose on 45 West Clinton Avenue. One of only two Romantic Octagons built in the United States, it is 50 feet in diameter. Each face of the octagonal core measures 20 feet, and each verandah side is 30 feet. The two-story core is original, while the two-story, slate-roofed dome with cupola was added about 1876.

Inside, the first floor comprises four large rectangular rooms in a cruciform shape, with four small triangular rooms between them. The large rooms include the entrance hall, living room, dining room, and kitchen, while the music room, pantry, and lavatories are wedge-shaped. Upstairs, five bedrooms and a study alternate with triangular bathrooms and closets. Designer Orson Squire Fowler was convinced that the octagonal form contributed to healthful living and economy of space. In *A Home for All,* he declared that "An unhandy house...by perpetually irritating mothers, sours the tempers of children even before birth, thus rendering the whole family bad-dispositioned by nature" (!)

> *"You could live in San Francisco a month and ask no greater entertainment than walking through it."*
> —Inez Hayes Irwin

THE PAINTED LADIES

The picturesque row of beautifully restored townhouses on San Francisco's Alamo Square exemplify the exuberance of the Queen Anne Revival style as expressed in the United States in the late nineteenth century. Featuring porches, railings, and eaves lavishly decorated with spindle- and spoolwork, finials, pendant gingerbread trim, floral and lacy motifs, and elaborate polychrome paintwork, these much-photographed homes are aptly described by the nickname "painted ladies."

Several American cities were expanding when the Queen Anne style was at its height, including San Francisco, whose Victorian houses are a national treasure. After the Gold Rush of 1849, a coherent grid plan was devised for the hilly site. Native redwood was the main building material, often milled and painted to resemble stone. A guide to the city in 1888 pointed out that "The superior facility for shaping wood, and the abundance of machinery for planing and molding, has led to the adoption of more architectural ornament here than in any other city."

Right: *A detail view of the terraced rooflines, varied window treatments, and gingerbread lace on San Francisco's Alamo Square.*

Overleaf: *Downtown San Francisco provides a stunning backdrop to the elegant Victorian townhouses.*

AT A GLANCE: ALAMO SQUARE

- San Francisco's "Postcard Row" is one of the nation's most photographed residential streets, its colorfully painted but stately Victorian houses contrasting sharply with the city skyline behind.
- The houses, built between the mid- and late nineteenth century, are excellent examples of the Queen Anne Revival style, their projecting gables, ornamental stickwork, and decorative porches being typical features.

SCHOOL

AT A GLANCE: BRADBURY BUILDING

- George Wyman, architect of The Bradbury Building, had no formal training and was employed as a junior draftsman when he was commissioned by tycoon Louis Bradbury to design a structure that would serve as the ageing mining tycoon's monument.
- The young architect used as his inspiration Edward Bellamy's 1887 novel *Looking Backward,* a futuristic tale set in 2000 that describes a utopian commercial building as "a vast hall of light" with a 100-foot-high dome and "walls frescoed in mellow tints."
- The Bradbury is most famous for its appearance in the 1982 science fiction movie *Blade Runner,* which portrays Los Angeles in the year 2019 as a futuristic dystopia.

> *"Take the Bradbury Building. It will make you famous"*
>
> —Mark Wyman

SOMEWHERE IN TIME

This ornament to the nineteenth-century core of Los Angeles, built in 1893 at 304 South Broadway, dates from the so-called Cast Iron Age in architecture, of which Chicago's contemporaneous Rookery Building is another outstanding example. As the section below and the photograph show, the design centers on a multistory inner glazed court furnished with elegant cast ironwork in the Art Nouveau style in the form of open stairways and elevator cages, as well as extensive balcony rails. In effect, the building turns its back on the busy street outside and treats the inner court as its façades, flooded with light from the glazed roof above. Still more surprising is the fact that this sophisticated design was the work of a young draftsman and builder who had originally worked in the office of architects Peters and Burns of Los Angeles and then for architect Sumner P. Hunt. When client Louis Bradbury rejected Hunt's plans for the office building, he offered the job to the thirty-two-year-old George Wyman, who astonished all concerned by producing this half-million-dollar landmark. It was inspired in part by Edward Bellamy's 1887 novel *Looking Backward,* which describes an idealized commercial building of the year 2000 as "a vast hall full of light."

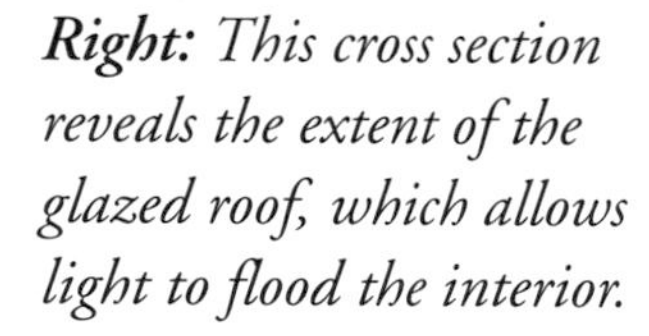

Right: This cross section reveals the extent of the glazed roof, which allows light to flood the interior.

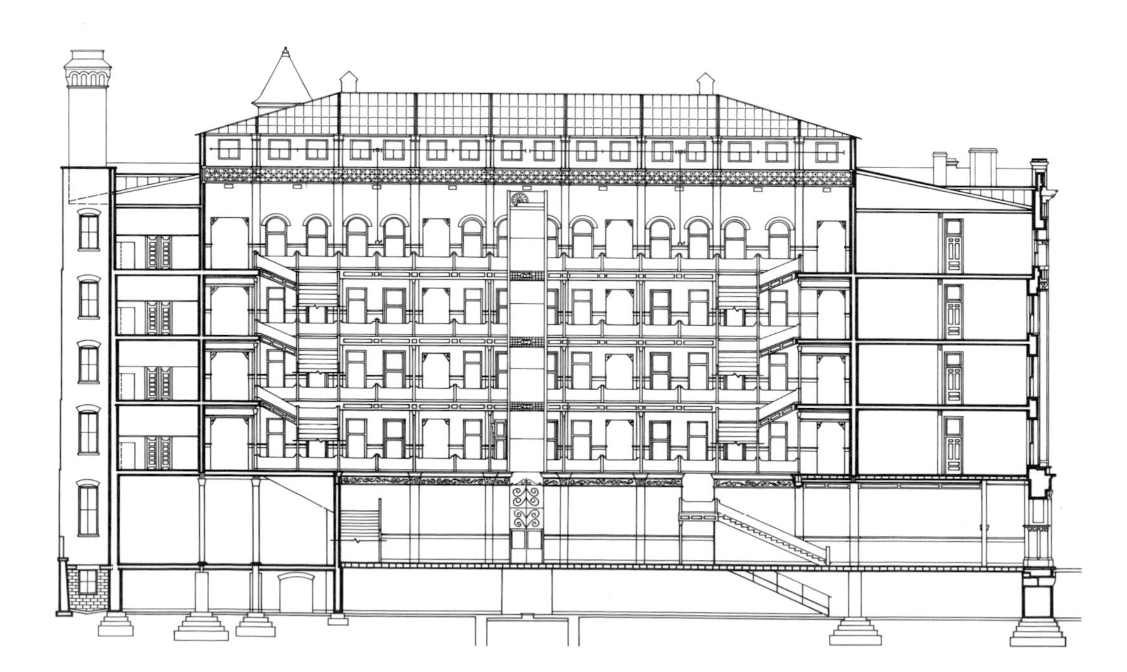

***Opposite:** The stairs and balcony rails are ornamented with Art Nouveau-style cast-iron work.*

"It is a lofty, soaring thing, rising in sheer exultation that from bottom to top it is a unit without a single dissenting line."
—Louis Sullivan

A PIONEERING SKYSCRAPER
This St. Louis landmark was commissioned to the Chicago firm of Dankmar Adler and Louis Sullivan in 1890. It is considered one of their masterpieces—the first tall building to be designed so that its steel framework is expressed in its exterior elevations. The clarity of its form and the richness of its ornament are features that placed Adler and Sullivan among the leaders of the Chicago School, along with Daniel H. Burnham, John Wellborn Root, and William Le Baron Jenney. All of these architects were deeply involved in the evolution of functional design for tall skeleton-framed buildings.

Sullivan's unique contribution was the intricate ornamentation that became known as Sullivanesque—a naturalistic but classically restrained decorative mode. Complex floral, foliar, and geometric ornament on both residential and commercial buildings set a new standard for Early Modern architecture, and, as Wright's mentor, Sullivan left an indelible impression on his work as we see it today.

AT A GLANCE: WAINWRIGHT BUILDING

- Completed in 1892, the Wainwright Building is one of the first examples of a modern skyscraper, with its steel skeleton bearing the weight that heavy, load-bearing walls shouldered in earlier versions. Other advances included elevators and a ventilation system.
- The design for the building came to Sullivan in a "sudden and volcanic" epiphany, while he was out walking.
- Once scheduled for demolition, the building was eventually spared this fate. It was declared a City of St. Louis Official Landmark in 1966.

"Make no little plans. They have no power to stir men's blood."
—Daniel Burnham

AT A GLANCE: RELIANCE BUILDING

- Chicago's Reliance Building, completed by Daniel Burnham in 1894, is a key prototype of the modern skyscraper. With its steel skeleton and tripartite plate glass windows, it is one of the most famous examples of the Chicago School of architecture.
- Soaring 200 feet above State Street, the building broke new ground in the architectural world. The thirteen upper levels were constructed at an amazing rate of one story every two days!
- The building's exterior is clad in highly glazed terra-cotta tiles, an innovation that would later be used to similar effect in the Wrigley Building (see pages 118–19) and New York City's Woolworth Building (page 104).

GLASS, STEEL, AND STONE

This important early skyscraper was the first to employ terra cotta for exterior surfacing. Architects Burnham and Root, whose firm had flourished in the rebuilding boom that followed the great Chicago fire of 1871, were responsible for the design. The lower story and mezzanine were completed in 1890, the upper thirteen stories in 1894. As summarized by the architectural historian Ada Louise Huxtable, "The famous Chicago window—a three-part projecting bay that created the extremely lively plastic façades of structures like the Tacoma and Reliance buildings...was a device to capture as much light and space as possible for the purpose of increasing the rental value of the offices. For most builders, there was minimal interest in dressing up the new curtain walls; the idea was to enclose the skeleton frame in the least costly fashion. These early structures are as handsome as they are utilitarian. They possess a great strength and clarity that gives them remarkable expressive power."

Left: Like many Chicago School skyscrapers, the Reliance Building's steel structure is anchored in bedrock concrete caissons more than 100 feet deep.

"Where we love is home, home that our feet may leave, but not our hearts."
—Oliver Wendell Holmes, Jr.

A BLUE RIDGE CHÂTEAU

George Washington Vanderbilt explored this hilltop site in North Carolina's Blue Ridge Mountains, near Asheville, in the late 1880s, but it is unlikely that he envisioned the family estate that would soon be established here. The Chateauesque-style mansion designed for Vanderbilt by Richard Morris Hunt is the most complete example of this style, as well as the largest private residence, in the United States. Its features include steeply pitched hipped roofs with many vertical elements, including spires, turrets, pinnacles, and decorative chimneys; multiple dormers, often extending through the cornice line,

***Right:** The steeply pitched roofline and lavish ornamentation reveal the influence of the* École des Beaux Arts *on Richard Morris Hunt, who was the first American architect to attend the school (1846).*

with steep parapeted gable roofs; and Gothic-style tracery or shallow relief carvings executed by master stone carvers. In fact, it took a thousand workmen and almost $5 million to build this 5-acre mansion, whose grounds were landscaped by Frederick Law Olmsted, the designer of New York City's Central Park.

Biltmore House has three kitchens, forty-three bathrooms, sixty-five fireplaces, and a library of c. 20,000 volumes. Now a museum of period architecture and decorative arts, its collection includes 70,000 objects ranging from Flemish tapestries, furniture by Chippendale and Sheraton, and fifty Persian and Oriental rugs, to paintings by Renoir, Sargent, and Whistler and a chess set that once belonged to Napoleon Bonaparte.

AT A GLANCE: THE BILTMORE ESTATE

- The 250-room Biltmore Estate is the nation's largest private residence. Built by George Vanderbilt in 1895, it was modeled after three sixteenth-century Renaissance châteaux in France's Loire Valley. Vanderbilt's descendants own the estate to this day.

- Originally, the mansion was set in 125,000 acres of land. Following her husband's sudden death, Edith Vanderbilt sold 87,000 of these to the federal government in 1915, which used the land to create the Pisgah National Forest.

- The estate brought economic prosperity to the Asheville area, with the founding of the Biltmore Forest School in 1898, the Biltmore Estate Industries in 1901, and Mrs. Vanderbilt's School for Domestic Science in 1903. Today, more than 900,000 people visit the estate each year.

"Do as I do—consult the spirits."
—Cornelius Vanderbilt

THE GILDED AGE

The opulent extravagance of Newport, Rhode Island, as the summer enclave of the rich and famous during the Gilded Age of American society, from about 1880 into the 1920s, has seldom been equaled anywhere. Fortunes were being amassed in transportation, finance, shipping, and other far-flung enterprises, and it became a point of honor for second- and third-generation tycoons to build a "summer cottage" (occupied only two months of the year) in styles ranging from French chateaux to Florentine palaces. Cornelius Vanderbilt II, a scion of the family whose

wealth was founded on the railroad and steamship enterprises of "Commodore" Cornelius Vanderbilt, chose the eminent architect Richard Morris Hunt to design his $7-million mansion "The Breakers"—the most imposing of all the houses along five-mile Bellevue Avenue, a street almost literally paved with gold. After extensive studies in Europe, Hunt had visited a brother in Newport and was soon in great demand as a palace-builder par excellence.

AT A GLANCE:
THE BREAKERS

- Originally a wooden house, purchased by Cornelius Vanderbilt II when he became Chairman and President of the New York Central Railroad System, The Breakers was destroyed by fire in 1892, the same year as the tragic death of Henry, the eldest Vanderbilt son.
- In 1893 Richard Morris Hunt designed the present seventy-room mansion in the style of an Italian Renaissance-style Palazzo. It cost $7 million and took 2,500 workers two years to build.
- The mansion takes its name from the waves that crash against the cliffs beneath. Its exquisite interiors include such features as the music room's gold ceiling, the dining room's rose-alabaster pillars, and a central courtyard that doubled as a ballroom.

The Breakers was modeled on several Roman villas of the Renaissance period that Hunt had studied near Genoa and Turin. Its materials included marbles and alabasters imported from Italy and Africa, Caen stone from France, and rare woods and mosaics from all over the world. The four-story façade measures 250 feet long, and the house has seventy rooms and thirty baths, as well as eleven acres of lawns and gardens. The galleried Great Hall rises 45 feet to a ceiling painted to resemble a cloud-swept sky. The most magnificent rooms include the library in a south wing; the grand salon, used for dancing and recitals; and the dining room, with its twelve monolithic pillars of rose alabaster, all furnished with art treasures of seven centuries acquired from around the world. The Breakers is now maintained by the Preservation Society of Newport County.

AT A GLANCE: PEWABIC POTTERY

- Pewabic Pottery was founded by Mary Chase Perry in 1903 at the height of the Arts and Crafts Movement. William B. Stratton (who would become Perry's husband in 1918) and Frank D. Baldwin designed and built the Tudor Revival building in 1907 when the pottery outgrew its first home—a stable.

- Perry became one of the nation's most influential ceramicists, and her work can be found in such diverse and distinguished places as the National Shrine of the Immaculate Conception in Washington, DC, and the Nebraska State Capitol.

- Perry was born in the Upper Michigan Peninsula copper country, and her workshop takes the name *Pewabic* from the Chippewa for "clay with a copper color." Spectacular iridescent glazes, among them green, rose, and copper, were her signature.

"[The Pottery's] idea has always been to...stamp this generation as one which brought about a revival of the ceramic arts and prove an inspiration to those who come after us."

—Mary Chase Perry Stratton

SALT OF THE EARTH

This sturdy Tudor Revival building, with its second-story overhang, hipped roof, and elaborate chimneys, is as characteristic of its time as the American art pottery that was made here. The exterior combination of stone and stucco with ornamental board trim emulated medieval timber construction, in which the exposed timbers served a structural purpose. The diamond-paned windows are also typical of this style, which enjoyed great popularity between 1900 and 1920.

"Nothing unimportant ever happens at the Plaza."
—From the Plaza Hotel's publicity

CENTRAL PARK LUXURY

This magnificent landmark in the French Renaissance style commands one of New York's grandest vistas from its location on Fifth Avenue and Central Park South (West 59th Street). It looks north to Central Park and east to Grand Army Plaza, with its splendid equestrian monument to Civil War general William T. Sherman and the famous five-tier Pulitzer Memorial Fountain. The hotel rises from a three-story marble base to a ten-story central section of light-colored brick capped by balustraded balconies, a massive cornice line, and a five-story mansard slate roof. Two corners are rounded to form symmetrical towers.

For almost a hundred years, The Plaza has been host to glittering parties, balls, and other social events, and its façade displays flags representing the countries of important foreign dignitaries and guests. Mr. and Mrs. Alfred Vanderbilt were first to sign the hotel register. Other illustrious guests include Ernest Hemingway and F. Scott Fitzgerald, whose novel *The Great Gatsby* features The Plaza as the meeting-place of its star-crossed lovers.

Recently renovated to its original luxurious state, The Plaza's amenities include the famous Oak Bar, with murals by Everett Shinn depicting scenes from around the hotel, and the Palm Court, with its imported Italian caryatids representing the four seasons. Also in this glamorous neighborhood are luxury hotels including the Ritz-Carlton, Inter-Continental, and Helmsley Park Lane, and local attractions include Lincoln Center, the Rockefeller Center, and exclusive shopping on Fifth Avenue.

AT A GLANCE: PLAZA HOTEL, NEW YORK CITY

- Conceived by a triumvirate of influential businessmen, the nineteen-story Plaza was designed by Henry Janeway Hardenbergh, creator of the Waldorf-Astoria and the Willard Intercontinental, in the opulent style of a French chateau.
- The Plaza opened on October 1, 1907, having taken two years and $12 million to build. A grand total of 1,650 crystal chandeliers illuminated its palatial interiors. Today its guests can enjoy, among other luxuries, an 8,000 square-foot spa facility.

AT A GLANCE: FLATIRON BUILDING

- New York's oldest skyscraper, the Flatiron Building was constructed in 1902 by Daniel Burnham. Named for his client, the Fuller Construction Company, the building's shape soon earned it the nickname it carries to this day.

- *Harper's Weekly* dubbed the structure "The Most Remarkable Building in the World." The building started a trend that spread across the nation; imitations were built and existing similar buildings were renamed or nicknamed "Flatiron."

- A strong updraft caused by the structure's aerodynamics made hats and skirts rise skyward with such predictability that crowds regularly gathered to watch unsuspecting passersby. According to New York legend the term "23 Skidoo" refers to the phrase used by police to alert each other of such gatherings.

***Right:** A view of the Flatiron Building from Madison Square Park, situated at the end of "Ladies Mile," once Manhattan's most fashionable shopping district.*

"[The building is] quite the most notorious thing in New York and attracts more attention than all the other buildings now going up together.... We have to congratulate the architect on the success of his detail."

—Architectural Record, 1902

IRON IN THE SOUL

This unmistakable skyscraper—New York City's first—was designed to occupy a narrow triangular lot created by the intersection of Broadway and Fifth Avenue at 23rd Street. It is twenty-one stories tall, and its steel framework is clad with rusticated limestone and molded terra cotta in the ornate style known as Renaissance Revival. From the narrow front view, it can be seen that the building resembles a Classical column. The first four stories are the base; the shaft rises in an unbroken line to the capital, or top, with its two-story arches and a heavy cornice that defines the roofline.

As seen in the quotation at left, other architects were favorably impressed by the building designed by their colleague Daniel H. Burnham, whose reputation in Chicago preceded him to New York. As an influential member of the Chicago School, he had designed one of the nation's first skyscrapers, the Monadnock Building, in 1891. The appropriately named Flatiron (originally Fuller) Building testifies to public perception of this unique skyscraper, which is still a much-loved New York landmark.

> *"Money, it turned out, was exactly like sex, you thought of nothing else if you didn't have it and thought of other things if you did."*
>
> —James Baldwin

AT A GLANCE: NEW YORK STOCK EXCHANGE

- Architect George B. Post's Greek Revival building opened in 1903, replacing an earlier five-story building that had served the Exchange since 1865.
- The building's pediment is its most distinctive feature and was designed by John Quincy Adams Ward. Its eleven sculpted figures are symbols of American commerce and industry.

PLACE YOUR STOCK IN US

Architect George B. Post was awarded the commission for this historic landmark on the basis of his competition-winning design. He chose the Greek Revival style, with a rusticated two-story base having rounded and arched openings. The base bears six Corinthian columns, behind which is a four-story glass curtain wall that admits light into the marble-walled trading room, with its 86-foot gilded ceiling.

The fine statuary in the imposing pediment (right), *Integrity Protecting the Works of Man,* was designed by J.Q.A.Ward and Paul Bartlett and carved in marble,which had to be replaced in 1936 due to New York City's air pollution. The figures were re-created in copper and lead coated to resemble stone. The building stands at 8 Broad Street, and its Wall Street entrance was planted with a historic buttonwood (sycamore) tree that commemorates the Buttonwood Agreement of May 1792, whereby twenty-four brokers who had been trading bonds drew up the document that formed the original board of the New York Stock Exchange.

AT A GLANCE: GAMBLE HOUSE

- Designed in 1908 by architects Charles and Henry Greene, the Gamble House is considered the nation's definitive Arts and Crafts-style house and embodies the highest stage of the California Bungalow Style.
- The Japanese influence, evidenced by the structure's low roofline and projecting eaves, derives from a visit by the brothers to the World's Columbian Exhibition, where they saw Japanese architecture for the first time.
- Built as a retirement residence for David Berry Gamble, a member of the Proctor and Gamble Company in Cincinnati, and his wife Mary, the house remained in the family until 1966 when it was bequeathed to the city of Pasadena.

"If you want a golden rule that will fit everything, this is it: Have nothing in your houses that you do not know to be useful or believe to be beautiful."
—William Morris

HOME IS WHERE THE ART IS

California architects Charles and Henry Greene established their successful practice in Pasadena and became known as the builders of "the ultimate bungalow," a style that was influenced by several factors, including the Japanese teahouse and the Swiss chalet. The Gamble House, with its low-pitched, multilevel rooflines, is constructed of wood and based entirely on craftsmanship principles, which the brothers had mastered in their studies at Calvin Woodward's experimental manual-training program sponsored by Washington University in St. Louis. The house is built mainly of redwood (Japanese carpenters were employed) and features rounded and polished rafters and an open plan extended by balconies and terraces. The Greenes oversaw every aspect of construction, fabricating most of their own hardware, decorative tiles, art-glass windows, and furniture, both built-in and movable. The interior glows with the luster of teak and mahogany.

AT A GLANCE: UNION STATION, WASHINGTON, DC

- The capital's railroad station was the biggest in the world upon its completion in 1908—so big, in fact, that the Washington Monument would fit horizontally within its concourse.
- The $125-million Beaux Arts-style building set the tone for marbled opulence throughout the capital, with the Lincoln and Jefferson Memorials making similar use of white granite grandeur.

"Electricity—carrier of light and power, devourer of time and space, bearer of human speech over land and sea, greatest servant of man, itself unknown."
—Charles W. Eliot, *Inscription,* Union Station, Washington, DC

GATEWAY TO THE CAPITAL

Derived from Charles Atwood's Classical railroad terminal built for the Chicago International Exposition of 1893 (often called the White City), Union Station was the work of architect Daniel H. Burnham, in collaboration with Charles F. McKim and sculptor Augustus Saint-Gaudens. The 663-foot-long façade consists of a central pavilion with three monumental arches set off by Corinthian columns and flanked by arcaded wings extending to arched pavilions. The barrel-vaulted Main Hall, with its mahogany benches and ticketing facilities, opened onto the grand concourse, 760 feet long and 130 feet wide. It was designed to serve all seven of the railroad lines entering the city in 1907. To emphasize the ever-growing power of the United States in world affairs, this gateway to the capital has a vast semicircular plaza with three flagpoles more than 100 feet tall surmounted by immense American eagles. The plaza's centerpiece is Lorado Taft's Columbus Memorial Fountain. Union Station has now been restored to its original splendor.

"A railroad is like a lie—you have to keep building it to make it stand."
—Mark Twain

A WORK OF GIANTS

The construction of the 2,000-mile transcontinental railroad is perhaps the greatest engineering feat in the nation's history. Certainly, no other project had to overcome so many grueling tests of endurance, so many problems in logistics. Union Pacific workers on the Great Plains, where trees were few and far between, had to dress timbers shipped from the East at great expense by rail and boat. Their counterparts on the Central Pacific, building east from San Francisco, had to drill and tunnel their way through the granite of the High Sierra. Salt Lake City, Utah, was the interim goal for junction of the two railroads, which took place in nearby Promontory in 1869. Salt Lake City's subsequent importance as a railroad intersection may be judged by the size and grandeur of the French Renaissance Revival-style terminal that opened here in 1909. The base is clad in dressed sandstone and the upper story in brick; the lavish detailing of the Mansard roofline includes circular dormers, gabled towers, and decorative ironwork. Stained-glass windows and murals adorn the main lobby.

AT A GLANCE:
UNION PACIFIC STATION, SALT LAKE CITY

- Dating from 1909, the Union Pacific Station was designed in the French Renaissance Revival Style, characterized by the steeply pitched Mansard roof with its inset dormers. Its lower story is clad in sandstone and the upper in brick.

- The Union Pacific Railroad was one of the largest and most ambitious engineering projects ever imagined. Spanning the entire continent, and crossing one river—the Weber—as many as thirty-one times, the only sizeable settlement on its 1,700-mile route was Salt Lake City.

AT A GLANCE: ROBIE HOUSE

- The Robie residence is a masterpiece of innovation. The built-in garage was the nation's first, and became a Wright signature. Steel beams supporting the vast roof, air-conditioning, and a central vacuum system were also significant technological advances.

- The eaves are the building's most distinctive external feature: they extend up to 20 feet beyond the external walls. A total of 174 art-glass windows and doors effectively transform the walls into screens that illuminate the house.

- Designated a National Historic Landmark in 1963, the house was donated to the University of Chicago in the same year by the development firm Webb and Knapp.

"At no point does [my work] involve denial of the elemental law and order inherent in all great architecture; rather, it is a declaration of love for the spirit of that law and order."

—Frank Lloyd Wright

BRAVE NEW WORLD

Called in its time "the House of the Century," Frank Lloyd Wright's best-known residence in the Prairie Style was designed for a narrow city lot in Chicago that still had a distant view of the prairielands beyond the city in 1906. The house was commissioned by a young inventor, Frederick C. Robie, who had requested a contemporary design that

would take advantage of the newest technology. Wright was given a free hand, and budget, in designing all the furnishings, plantings, and utility systems.

The long, low structure is built entirely of brick and concrete, free of ornamentation, if we except the square concrete courses that accentuate the horizontal design of the house. The various porches and balconies that provide access to the outdoors on several levels have been compared to the prows and decks of a ship. Inside (main floor, see above), the Robie House was revolutionary in having no walls or partitions to break the flow of space through the common areas: living room, dining room, and central stairwell. This space continues into diamond-shaped bays at either end of the house, which open onto porches. The bedrooms, kitchen, and servants' quarters were placed at the rear of the house. The textiles, furnishings, and art-glass doors and windows are all of Wright's design, and the Robie House cost the then-prohibitive sum of $60,000. Many consider this house the highest achievement of what has been called Wright's First Golden Age.

Above: *The classical proportions of the living room show Wright's genius for reinterpreting the past in ways that were relevant to twentieth-century needs.*

GRAND CENTRAL
TERMINAL

> *"We've all heard that it's too late, that [the demolition] has to happen, but we know that's not so!"*
> —Jacqueline Kennedy Onassis

AT A GLANCE: GRAND CENTRAL TERMINAL

- A masterpiece of Beaux Arts design, Grand Central Terminal replaced a smaller predecessor at the massive cost of $43 million. Even in 1913 the city's real-estate prices were astronomical, necessitating construction of the vast train yard underground.

- The colossal project involved the removal of 3 million cubic yards of rock and earth and 200 buildings to make way for the new terminal. Construction projects above the terminal's tracks, including the Waldorf Astoria Hotel, were assessed "air rights," allaying the station's building costs.

- Controversial plans to adapt or even demolish the building have surfaced over the years. Among the most spectacular was a plan in the mid-1960s to top the station with a huge skyscraper, foiled by the ardent protests of campaigners including former First Lady Jacqueline Kennedy Onassis.

JEWEL IN THE CROWN

Architects Warren and Wetmore collaborated with Reed & Stem to produce this imposing structure, which was financed by Cornelius Vanderbilt's New York Central Railroad. Its steel-frame construction is clad in granite and limestone, and the 42nd Street façade (opposite) has three grand arches framed with Doric columns grouped in pairs. The 13-foot central clock is surrounded by Jules Coutan's sculptures of *Mercury, Hercules,* and *Miranda.* The terminal's expansive grand concourse, recently renovated, is 120 feet wide and 275 feet long.

AT A GLANCE: WOOLWORTH BUILDING

- Originally billed as a 625-foot, $5-million structure, the Woolworth Building soared in both height and cost to an eventual 792 feet and $13.5 million.

- On April 24, 1913, President Woodrow Wilson activated the interior and exterior illuminations, marking the opening of the building. On the same day, Reverend S. Parkes Cadman, a popular minister, coined the phrase "the Cathedral of Commerce."

"I decided to erect a building that would advertise the Woolworth 5 and 10 cent stores all over the world."
—Frank W. Woolworth

CATHEDRAL OF COMMERCE

The Woolworth Building, designed by the eminent architect Cass Gilbert for retail magnate Frank W. Woolworth, was under construction for three years, and its cost—$13.5 million—was paid in cash. Designed in the graceful Gothic Revival style, the sixty-story skyscraper has a thirty-story base and a thirty-story tower capped by a pyramidal roof clad in copper. Even today, its silhouette is unmistakable in the crowded New York City skyline. At 792 feet high, it was the city's tallest building for almost twenty years. Framed in structural steel, it is covered with terra cotta from the fourth floor up. Gothic detailing of cream-colored terra cotta includes the traditional flying buttresses, pinnacles, and sculptured gargoyles, which had been adopted from medieval architecture during the nineteenth century. Many of the city's older buildings are ornamented with both functional gargoyles, which serve as rainspouts, and grotesques, which serve a purely decorative purpose. Two amusing features of this landmark were designed for the lobby by Thomas R. Johnson: a bas-relief of Woolworth counting his nickels and dimes and a caricature of Cass Gilbert studying a model of the building.

"No money, artistic or architectural skill will be spared in making the edifice a monumental advertisement for Seattle and the Northwest"
—Lyman C. Smith

AT A GLANCE: SMITH TOWER

- Built at a cost of $1 million, the building's original plans were quite modest. Burns Lyman Smith, heir to the fortune, persuaded his father that a taller building would generate publicity for the company, so the design was redrawn.

- Completed in 1914 and opened on Independence Day of that year, Seattle's Smith Tower, named for typewriter tycoon Lyman C. Smith, was at the time the second-tallest structure in the nation and the fourth-tallest in the world.

PUGET SOUND'S GUIDING LIGHT

One of Seattle's most interesting buildings, the historic Smith Tower, stands at Yesler Way and Second Avenue. It was designed for the entrepreneur Lyman C. Smith (of Smith-Corona typewriters) by architects Gaggin & Gaggin and became for many years the tallest building (forty-two stories) west of the Mississippi River. It remained Seattle's tallest building until 1969. The first local owner, Ivan Haglund, acquired the tower in 1976. He raised a flag atop the tower depicting a carp, a symbol of his seafood-restaurant empire. Smith Tower is now part of Seattle's Pioneer Square Historic District, which recalls the city's lumbering industry: it was originally known as "Skid Roll" because logs were rolled down to the water here (this is the origin of the expression "Skid Row"). Nearby places of interest include the original Pike Place Market, built in 1907, and the Pioneer Building, designed by Elmer Fisher in 1890.

***Left:** Smith Tower was constructed with a steel frame and clad in terra cotta. The observation deck is 400 feet above ground level, and the pyramidal steepletop above it originally contained a water tank with a 15,000-gallon capacity.*

AT A GLANCE: AHWAHNEE HOTEL

- *Ahwahnee* was the name given to the Yosemite Valley by the Ahwahneechee, who lived there before the outstandingly beautiful area was "discovered" in the 1850s.
- The hotel was designed by Gilbert Stanley Underwood, whose work for the National Parks Service includes lodges at their Bryce Canyon, Zion, Sun Valley, Mount Hood, and Grand Canyon sites—all landmarks in their own right.
- Architectural features harmonizing the building with its surroundings include the ingenious use of colored concrete to simulate natural wood, and the stepping-up of stone masses, imitating the sheer valley walls surrounding the structure.
- A combination of earthquakes and glaciers created the majestic cliffs and waterfalls that draw visitors to *Ahwahnee*.

"On entering The Ahwahnee one is conscious of calm and complete beauty echoing the mood of majesty and peace that is the essential quality of Yosemite...against a background of forest and precipice the architect has nestled the great structure of granite, scaling his design with sky and space and stone."

—Ansel Adams

PEACE IN THE VALLEY

Skillfully designed to blend into its beautiful environment, rather than to obtrude upon it, the historic Ahwahnee Hotel bears the imprint of architect Gilbert Underwood, whose conservationist convictions are reflected in his various lodges for the National Park Service. California's Yosemite National Park was created in 1890 due chiefly to the influence of the eminent naturalist John Muir.

"A monument to the skill and faithful performance of workers on the rolls of the Works Progress Administration."
—Inscription, Timberline Lodge

A LABOR OF LOVE

Timberline Lodge was one of the most significant Works Progress Administration projects undertaken in Oregon. Built 1936–37 in the dramatic setting of Mount Hood, the state's highest peak, the steeply pitched rooflines and local materials are elements that contribute to an overall design in perfect harmony with the surroundings (its architects dubbed the style "Cascadian," for the mountain range). This is a regional expression of the Shingle style in resort architecture that was popular during the early twentieth century.

AT A GLANCE: TIMBERLINE LODGE

- Timberline Lodge was one of America's most ambitious public employment projects, built at the height of the Great Depression by unemployed craftspeople hired by the Federal Works Progress Administration.
- The project was completed in an astoundingly short time; just fourteen months passed from groundbreaking in June 1936 until President Franklin D. Roosevelt's dedication in September 1937.
- The Lodge was declared a National Historic Landmark in 1978. Its imposing exterior was immortalized in Stanley Kubrick's 1980 horror classic *The Shining.*
- Mount Hood is a volcano that could erupt catastrophically, but has been quiet for almost 200 years.

AT A GLANCE: WOODBURY COUNTY COURTHOUSE

- The courthouse is one of the largest Prairie-school structures in the nation. The building's dramatic horizontal planes, Roman brick exterior, and terra-cotta trim are elements that reflect the wide, open landscape of the prairies.
- Originally designed in the Gothic Revival style by architect William LaBarth Steele, a former employee at Louis Sullivan's Chicago offices, the design was completed in collaboration with George G. Elmslie and William G. Purcell, whose input transformed the project.
- The courthouse cost $825,641 to build, and was recently awarded $300,000 for preservation by Save America's Treasures, a public-private partnership of the White House Millennium Council and the National Trust for Historic Preservation.

"Our liberties we prize, our rights we will maintain."
—Iowa state motto, inscribed above rotunda stairway

"In breadth, length, height and weight, these buildings belonged to the prairie just as the human being himself belonged to it with his gift of speed."
—Frank Lloyd Wright

STATE OF THE ART

Constructed between 1916 and 1918, the Woodbury County Courthouse in Sioux City, Iowa, is the only large civic structure in the Prairie-school style. This is due to the input of architects George G. Elmslie and William G. Purcell, whose influence prevailed over the original Gothic Revival building planned by architect William Steele. The courthouse reflects the tenets of Frank Lloyd Wright, who originated the Prairie style as a horizontal building, often multilevel, with wide sheltering eaves and materials in harmony with their natural surroundings. His was a new concept of space that is reflected in dozens of Midwestern houses and in buildings like this, created by admirers of the style, including many architects who had worked with him in Chicago and in Oak Park, Illinois. The courthouse is notable for its cladding of tan Roman brick with matching terra-cotta trim, for bands of vertical windows separated by pilasters, and for the sculptural figures above the main entrances. The two-story building has a central office tower rising another six stories to an interior rotunda with a stained glass dome, lavishly ornamented with Sullivanesque-style designs in terra cotta and murals by artist John W. Norton.

OUR RIGHTS WE WILL MAINTAIN
OUR LIBERTIES WE PRIZE

***Below and opposite:** The sunbursts on the library's tower pyramid and the rotunda ceiling symbolize the "light of learning," a theme that pervades the design. The library has served Los Angeles since 1926.*

THE LIGHT OF LEARNING

Architect Bertram Goodhue's theme for this inspiring and eclectic public building was "the light of learning," and the theme is carried out in myriad ways. The famous Globe Chandelier, suspended in the Lodwrick M. Cook Rotunda, was designed by Goodhue Associates and modeled by Lee Lawrie. Nine feet in diameter, it is made of cast bronze at an original cost of $40,000. A model of the solar system, there are planets and a crescent moon in the chains, and the sunburst on the ceiling mirrors the pyramidal sunburst that crowns the library. Other ornaments to this civic monument include the vividly painted ceiling by Renee Petropoulos in the first-floor lobby, Lee Lawrie's Statue of Civilization flanked by its guardian sphinxes in black Belgian marble with bronze headdresses, and landscape architect Lawrence Halprin's Grotto Fountain,

with artworks by Jud Fine. As Fine describes it, "The Public Library as a principle is our most important democratic institution. It answers the demand for education for one and all, providing an accessible knowledge base for social and cultural progression."

"I have always imagined that Paradise will be a kind of library."
—Jorge Luis Borges

AT A GLANCE: LOS ANGELES PUBLIC LIBRARY

- Designed by Bertram Goodhue, with Carlton M. Winslow, Sr., supervising, the Los Angeles Public Library was inspired by Goodhue's masterpiece, the Nebraska State Capitol.

- A unique blend of architectural styles influenced Goodhue's design. The central tower, for example, is capped by a pyramid, referring to Egypt's legendary library at Alexandria, one of the Seven Wonders of the Ancient World.

- Symbolic motifs throughout the building reflect the architect's visionary commitment to its function. These include Lee Lawrie's Statue of Civilization and her sculpted finial atop the tower pyramid—a golden hand, entwined by the Serpent of Knowledge, clasping the Light of Learning (the original sculpture was recently replaced by a replica).

ANTENNA

Originally planned as a mooring mast for zeppelins, the tower's apex now serves both as a communications antenna and a lightning conductor.

OBSERVATION DECKS

More than 100 million visitors have admired the view from observatories on the 86th and 102nd stories.

DECORATED SETBACKS

The tower's Art Deco-style setbacks serve to accentuate its height and to allow more light to reach the streets beneath.

FLOODLIGHTS

The upper stories of the tower (from the 72nd story) are floodlit nightly, with colors used for special occasions.

STAIRS

More than 1,800 steps extend from the lobby to the 102nd floor. Athletes in the annual Empire State Run-up race up the stairs to the 86th story, the record time being just under 10 minutes—less than 7 seconds per story.

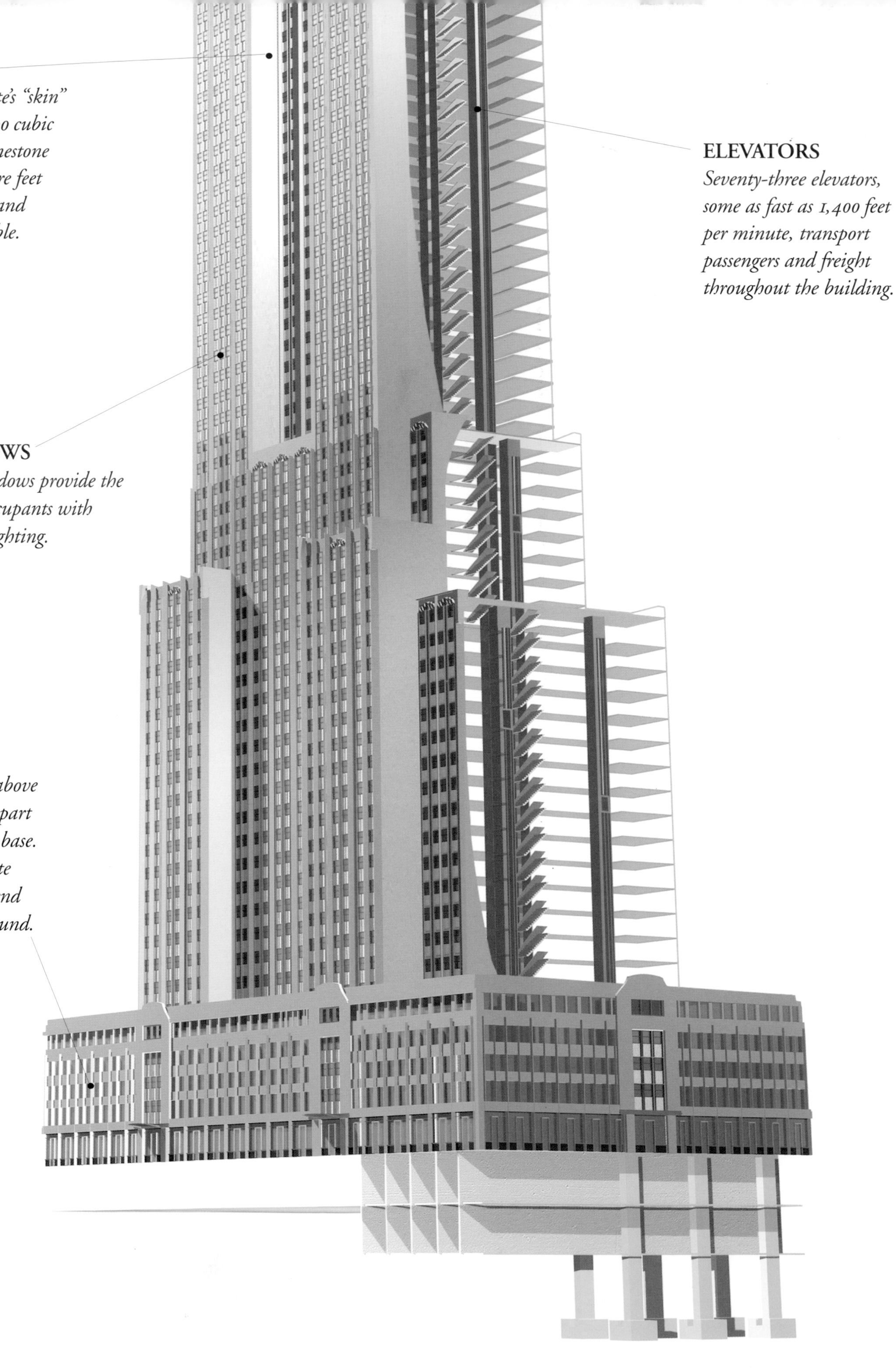
MASONRY
The Empire State's "skin" comprises 200,000 cubic feet of India Limestone and 10,000 square feet of Rose Famosa and Estrallante marble.
ELEVATORS
Seventy-three elevators, some as fast as 1,400 feet per minute, transport passengers and freight throughout the building.
WINDOWS
6,500 windows provide the tower's occupants with natural lighting.
BASE
The five stories above street level form part of the building's base. Steel and concrete foundations extend 55 feet below ground.

"When I'm in New York I look at the Empire State Building and feel as though it belongs to me . . . or is it vice versa?"
—Fay Wray

SYMBOL OF MANHATTAN

Recognized around the world, the streamlined silhouette of this remarkable landmark was the inspiration of architects Shreve, Lamb & Harmon, who were commissioned to design "something big" by developer John J. Raskob and Alfred E. Smith, the former four-term governor of New York, the Empire State. The building rose rapidly on the former site of the Waldorf Astoria Hotel, despite the onset of the Great Depression in October 1929. As Paul Goldberger observes in *The Skyscraper* (Knopf, 1981), comparing it with the Chrysler Building, "It is more restrained and dignified, and just as handsome. The limestone, nickel, aluminum, and granite of the façade create a streamlined, grayish tone that is appropriate for both New York and for the idea of height, and there is just the right hint of Art Deco ornament. The five-story base, for its part, holds the street line well and assures that the huge bulk of the tower is at a soft visual and psychological distance from passersby." Two years after its completion, the Empire State Building was immortalized by the movie *King Kong*, starring Fay Wray and the gigantic gorilla who attempted to escape his tormenters by climbing to the building's rounded tower and fending off the biplanes sent to attack him. Until the ill-fated World Trade Center Towers were completed in 1973, the Empire State was the world's tallest skyscraper. It was declared a National Historical Landmark in 1986. Virtual visitors can now enjoy the spectacular views from the top via the building's webcam.

AT A GLANCE: EMPIRE STATE BUILDING

- The 1,454-foot-high, 103-story Empire State building cost $40,948,900 and was constructed in a record-breaking one year and forty-five days, or 7 million man hours.
- The building serves as a huge lightning rod for the surrounding area and is struck approximately 100 times each year. Electricity is dissipated through the 60,000-ton steel skeleton and diffused into the ground below.
- Static buildup can cause St. Elmo's Fire to stream from the fingertips of rooftop visitors and sparks to fly from kissing lovers.
- One of the world's most photographed and photogenic structures, it has appeared in scores of movies including *King Kong* (1933), *An Affair to Remember* (1957), *Manhattan* (1979), and *Sleepless in Seattle* (1993).

"Everybody wonders about the Castle—why it is and what it is. That's what we wonder too... It's not nearly finished and maybe never will be. We don't know. We build as fancy leads."
—Bessie Johnson

FAR AND AWAY

An unlikely friendship between a Chicago millionaire in uncertain health and a larger-than-life roughneck horse wrangler nicknamed "Death Valley Scotty" resulted in this handsome concrete castle with its red-tiled roofline, patios, outbuildings,

Right: *A detail of the thick-walled Moorish arches and parapets that connect various parts of the sprawling hacienda.*

Opposite: *A view of the Mediterranean-style clock tower with chimes beyond the inner courtyard.*

Overleaf: *"Scotty's Castle" rises like a mirage from the arid isolation of Death Valley National Monument. Like Topsy, the complex "just grew" over a period of years, beginning in 1922.*

and ornaments united by a Spanish Mediterranean motif. It rose in Inyo County, California, in what was then called Grapevine Canyon, as a refuge from Chicago's freezing winters for Albert M. Johnson, president of the National Life Insurance Company of America, and his wife, Bessie. Mr. Johnson suffered a broken back as the result of a train wreck at the height of his career and was invited to Death Valley for his health by the flamboyant Walter Perry Scott, whom he had met in Chicago. Scott was known as a sometime gold prospector and full-time self-promoter, who kept himself in the public eye for decades with such stunts as disrupting railroad schedules and riding hard down Main Street handing out gold coins and $100 tips to newsboys. Despite their total dissimilarity in temperament, the two men were enamored of the desert and enjoyed the contrast between soaring Mount Whitney, rising more than 14,000 feet on the horizon, and nearby Bad Water, 279 feet below sea level, with its record-breaking temperatures of up to 135 degrees. Here, under the auspices of designer Charles Alexander MacNeilledge, the hacienda took shape, its principal materials comprising redwood, imported ceramic tile, stucco finishes, and handwrought metalwork. Much of the work was done by European craftsmen, and art treasures from many lands were used for the furnishings. As completed, Death Valley Ranch has twenty-one oversize main rooms, a handsomely tiled courtyard resembling those of the California missions, eight master baths, six large fireplaces, and a music wing, as well as stables and guest houses. The complex is now owned and administered by the National Park Service and is one of the most-visited tourist attractions in the Far West.

AT A GLANCE: DEATH VALLEY RANCH

- Death Valley Ranch, popularly known as "Scotty's Castle," was built in the style of a hacienda as a vacation retreat for the eccentric Chicago millionaire Albert Mussey Johnson.

- Construction commenced in 1922 but various setbacks delayed completion. Following the great stock-market crash of 1929, Johnson lost his fortune and construction was halted, leaving many of the projects unfinished.

- "Scotty's" takes its name from the flamboyant self-publicist, prospector, and confidence trickster Walter P. Scott, who formed a lifelong friendship with Johnson and remained on the ranch after Johnson's death.

MORE THAN A SKYSCRAPER
One of Chicago's premier buildings since its construction (1920–24) is the distinctive Wrigley Building, designed by architects Graham, Anderson, Probst and White. The building was commissioned by William Wrigley, Jr., as headquarters for his succesful chewing-gum business, and many other enterprises quickly sought space in the new towers of commerce rising on Michigan Avenue along the north bank of the Chicago River. The roughly triangular site purchased by Wrigley presented a challenge that his architects, including the chief designer, Charles Beersman, resolved in an ingenious way.

"And each time I leave,
Chicago is Tuggin' my sleeve,
Chicago is The Wrigley Building..."
—Frank Sinatra, *My Kind of Town (Cahn/vanHeusen)*

The building consists of two sections—north and south—connected at street level by an arcaded walkway and by enclosed walkways at the third- and fourteenth-floor levels. The two buildings comprise roughly 500,000 square feet of floor space, and the south section was already fully rented upon its completion in April 1921. The south, or clock-tower, section soars to 425 feet or thirty stories—nine stories higher than its counterpart. A Chicago landmark for almost seventy years, the clock itself is two stories high and has four dials more than 19 feet in diameter.

The building's ornamental designs and gleaming white exterior are an American adaptation of the then-popular French Renaissance style. It was clad in a special glazed terra cotta, which is periodically hand-washed to preserve its pristine appearance. The Wrigley Plaza (added 1957) adjoins Michigan Avenue between the two sections of the building, creating a green oasis of trees and fountains in this now densely developed part of Chicago, where the foundations of Modern architecture were laid by Louis Sullivan, Daniel H. Burnham, and other far-sighted builders.

AT A GLANCE: WRIGLEY BUILDING

- The Wrigley Building was constructed in 1920–24 as a headquarters for the successful chewing-gum business of William Wrigley, Jr., and was the first office building in Chicago's now-teeming North Michigan Avenue business district.
- The building comprises two sections joined by skywalks and houses almost 500,000 square feet of office space. This structure provides maximum natural light to the workspace.
- Inspired by Seville Cathedral, Spain, the building's clock tower soars 425 feet above the busy streets. The gleaming white terra-cotta exterior is hand-washed by a specialist crew.

AT A GLANCE: FOX THEATER, ATLANTA

- Named for William Fox, founder and president of Fox Studios, the theater is one of few surviving examples of 500 movie palaces he owned at the peak of his empire.
- The 4,000-seat theater was originally designed as the Yaarab Temple Shrine Mosque, home of the Shriner organization. Its minarets and onion domes, complemented by lavish and opulent interiors, give the structure a palatial ambience.
- The building was declared a National Historic Landmark in 1976 and has since undergone a $20-million renovation program. An in-house restoration team tends to the building's treasures, and it continues to prosper as an arts complex.

"No second of every 24 hours passes but that the name of William Fox is on the screen in some part of the world."
—William Fox

THE FABULOUS FOX

Harking back to the lavish and exotic décor of Hollywood's first Golden Age theaters, the Fox Theater in Atlanta, Georgia, has been described as "beautifully outlandish, opulent, grandiose…[a] monument to the heady excesses of the pre-crash 1920s." Its huge auditorium lacked nothing in Oriental splendor, from an indoor Arabian courtyard with a sky full of flickering stars and "drifting" clouds to Moorish tiles, ornate grillework, and canopies lavished with rhinestones and sequins. A true survivor, the theater has outlasted the Great Depression, television, suburban flight, and threats of demolition to be restored to its former splendor by an army of volunteers augmented by skilled artisans dedicated to the slogan "Fix the Fox." Today, the revitalized movie palace and cultural center generates millions of dollars for Atlanta's economy.

> *"Miami Beach is where neon goes to die."*
> —Lenny Bruce

TURN OF THE CENTURY

Located at 140 Ocean Drive in Miami Beach, Florida, the Century Hotel is an excellent example of Miami Beach Art Deco, designed in 1939 by architect Henry Hohauser. It has been fully restored and has received numerous coveted awards, including the Miami Design Preservation League's award for outstanding façade preservation. It reflects the history of south Florida's real-estate boom of the early 1900s, which went bust during the Great Depression, ending plans for making "the Beach"—originally a mangrove-swamp island separating Biscayne Bay from the Atlantic—a kind of Palm Beach South for the super-rich. When new construction resumed in the late 1930s, Miami Beach was redesigned to attract more middle-class vacationers for one- or two-week stays. Multicolored pastel hotels like the Century sprang up along Ocean Park and Drive in the streamlined Art Deco style, with decoratively scalloped trim, portholes that suggested ocean liners, streamlined or hard-edged corners, and central stepped ornaments above the entryways. The resort flourished for several decades before many of the ageing hotels became boarding houses for retirees on limited incomes. A citywide program of restoration has renewed many of these buildings to their original whimsical, off-beat charm, contributing to the renaissance of Miami Beach as a vibrant, cosmopolitan vacation destination. Other hotels designed here by Hohauser include the Essex House (1938), which features porthole windows and a neon tower; the streamlined Cardozo (1939); the Henry Hotel (1939); and the recently restored Penguin Hotel (1949).

AT A GLANCE: CENTURY HOTEL, MIAMI

- A beautiful example of Art Deco architecture, The Century was designed in 1939 by the prolific architect Henry Hohauser, creator of more than 300 buildings in the area and fondly nicknamed the "father of Miami Beach Art Deco."
- The term "Art Deco" derives from the 1925 Paris *Exposition Internationale des Arts Decoratifs Industriels et Modernes*. The Century's sleek, streamlined façade, with its central column suggestive of an Egyptian motif, make it a fine example of the style.
- The building was renovated extensively in 1997, with such modernizations as digital television and high-speed Internet access renewing both its appearance and its name.

"Every industry should establish its own technical museum for the inspiration of others in industry, the study of its clients, and the general education of the public, and they should not only cover history, but present products and possibilities for the future."
—John Woodman Higgins

IN SHINING ARMOR

Located in Worcester, Massachusetts, this singular landmark evolved from the private collection of the industrialist John Woodman Higgins, who searched the world for arms and armor before building this Art-Deco style building with rich Gothic interiors to house it. He obtained a charter for a museum of historical and

modern metal artifacts in 1929. The Armory's Western collection includes 3,000 armors and components, 1,000 weapons and accessories, and hundreds of swords, daggers, firearms, stained glass, and wood carvings. The non-Western collection is similarly comprehensive, containing artifacts from Africa, the Islamic world, India, and Japan.

AT A GLANCE: HIGGINS ARMORY MUSEUM

- Believed to be America's first building composed entirely of steel and glass, the museum was constructed by industrialist John Woodman Higgins as a home for his vast collection of arms and armor.

- Designed by Boston architect Joseph D. Leland, the four-story L-shaped building cost over $300,000. Its magnificent Gothic-style interiors were inspired by visits to Europe, and its vaulted ceilings based on Austria's Hohenwerfen Castle.

- On Higgins's death in 1961 the museum, containing over 6,000 exhibits, was left to the public. Designated a National Historic Landmark in 1980, a multimillion-dollar restoration and modernization campaign has since preserved its treasures for many generations to come.

AT A GLANCE: CINCINNATI MUSEUM CENTER

- Formerly Cincinnati's Union Terminal, the building is one of the nation's most famous Art Deco structures. Initially designed by New York architects Alfred Fellheimer and Stewart Wagner, the building was planned originally in a classical style.

- Beaux Arts graduate Paul Philippe Cret was hired as a consultant in 1930 and redesigned the building significantly. His other work includes buildings at the University of Texas, the Detroit Institute of the Arts, and interiors for the Pioneer Zephyr trains.

- Completed in 1933, the Terminal was a huge success. Up to 20,000 passengers per day passed through here during World War II, when it was a transfer point for soldiers. The decline in train travel ended its career as a terminal in 1972, and it lay empty until 1990, when it reopened as a museum.

"The complaint...about modern steel furniture, modern glass houses, modern red bars and modern streamlined trains and cars is that all these objets modernes, *while adequate and amusing in themselves, tend to make the people who use them look dated."*

—Elwyn Brooks

THE END OF THE LINE

French-American architect Paul Philippe Cret was the major influence on this significant Art Deco building, which despite its modernistic look is imbued with the classical proportions of the Beaux-Arts design principles that he espoused. After emigrating from Lyons to Philadelphia in 1903, his career as an architect and educator gained great momentum during the 1920s and '30s, when he designed this handsome railroad terminal and other civic and memorial buildings in a modernized classical style adapted to new steel-frame construction. Cret's other work includes the Folger Shakespeare Library in Washington, DC (1929), the noted Philadelphia Rodin Museum (1928), and the Federal Reserve Building, located in the nation's capital (1935). In 1938 the importance of Paul Philippe Cret's work was recognized with the American Institute of Architects' Gold Medal.

Right: *The façade of the Union Terminal, with its superb Art Deco features, was beautifully restored during the building's conversion to its new use.*

Left: *Many critics assert that this famous tower is the most attractive expression of the Art Deco style in the world.*

"A bold structure declaring the glories of the modern age."
— Walter Chrysler

ART DECO MASTERPIECE

An Art Deco monument to the great automobile age, the seventy-seven-story Chrysler Building was commissioned to architect William Van Alen by industrialist Walter P. Chrysler. Setbacks in tall buildings had recently become part of New York City's building laws, and the Chrysler Building shows a creative use of what might have been a limitation. The building's five setbacks contribute to a harmonious whole that combines white ceramic brick with futuristic ornaments of a chromium-nickel steel alloy never used before in an American building. The fourth setback (26th floor) features automobile patterns in white and grey brick and 10-foot-high winged radiator caps.

The competitive Van Alen had a surprise up his sleeve when the Chrysler Building was nearing completion. He had its 185-foot spire assembled secretly in the dome and raised to the peak so as to surpass the height of the 927-foot Bank of Manhattan, just completed by his former partner and rival H. Craig Severance. Thus the Chrysler Building, at 1,046 feet, had its day in the sun as the world's tallest building—only until the Empire State Building surpassed it shortly thereafter. The Chrysler Building's lobby is a study in multicolored marble and granite, with ceiling murals by Edward Trumbull depicting world commerce and industry, and elevator doors and walls inlaid with Art Deco motifs in exotic woods.

AT A GLANCE: THE CHRYSLER BUILDING

- Upon its completion in 1930, the Chrysler Building was the tallest structure in the world, at 1,046 feet and seventy-seven stories, for just a few months before being overreached by the new Empire State Building.
- The structure contains almost 4 million bricks, 500,000 tiles, 20,961 tons of steel, and 112,000 square feet of marble wainscot.
- The eagle gargoyles adorning the four corners of the fifty-ninth floor are massive replicas of the hood ornament on the 1929 model of the Chrysler Plymouth.
- The building's characteristic sunburst design and Art Deco gargoyles adorning its upper stories are constructed of the innovative Nirosta® chromium-nickel steel—the first use of the alloy in an American building.

"I had no ambition to make a fortune. Mere money-making has never been my goal, I had an ambition to build."
—John D. Rockefeller

AT A GLANCE: ROCKEFELLER CENTER

- The Rockefeller Center, constructed between 1931 and 1940 as a commercial and entertainment development, was originally to be called "Radio City." Comprised of fourteen skyscrapers, with open plazas and walkways, it remains the largest private building project ever undertaken in the United States.

- The theme of human progress pervades the complex, with such sculptures as Paul Manship's *Prometheus* and Lee Lawrie's *Atlas* epitomizing the optimistic and tenacious spirit of the age, blending classical motifs with Art Deco styling.

- Despite technological innovations like underground parking, the complex did not achieve its potential until the installation of a skating rink in the sunken plaza, which transformed the space into one of the city's top attractions.

A MODERN CLASSIC

This National Historic Landmark was the first development in which skyscrapers were designed as a group. Initially, the site was planned as a venue for New York City's Metropolitan Opera House, but after the stock market crash of 1929, the Opera House withdrew from the project and its focus shifted to a mixed business center—still the world's most extensive privately owned business and entertainment complex. A consortium of three architectural firms worked with developer John D. Rockefeller, Jr.: Hood, Godley & Fouilhoux; Corbett, Harrison & MacMurray; and Reinhard & Hofmeister.

The focal point of the Rockefeller Center is the GE Building (illustrated opposite), originally the RCA Building. This tall limestone tower ascends from a 4-foot granite base to a height of 850 feet. The combination of high and low buildings, gardens, and plazas, creates the sense of orderly openness that prevails here. The center is home to Radio City Music Hall, the Rainbow Room, and the NBC broadcasting Studios, along with a host of other business and entertainment facilities, including the famous winter ice-skating plaza.

Left: *This dramatic perspective showing part of the Rockefeller Center gives an idea of the highly ambitious scale of the complex.*

Opposite: *The primary building of the Center is an impressive Art Deco landmark in itself.*

AT A GLANCE: CRANBROOK ACADEMY OF ART

- The Academy of Art is part of the Cranbrook Foundation, founded by newspaper magnate George Booth and his wife Ellen and inspired by the American Academy in Rome. Its vision is to "add and strengthen the educational and cultural facilities within the state of Michigan."
- The Academy's educational model was based upon the ancient European working practice of master and apprentice. A community of artists and their students lived on campus, close to their studios and workshops.
- The building was designed and built by Finnish-American architect Eliel Saarinen, its first president, in 1942.

"We wished to see our dreams come true while we were, to the best of our ability, helping to carry on the work of creation."
—George Booth

A QUIET GRANDEUR

Eliel Saarinen was already a well-established European architect when he submitted his design for the Chicago Tribune Tower in 1922. It won second prize, and he emigrated to the United States a year later to continue his glittering career. His influential school of art and design, in Bloomfield Hills, Michigan, attracted many talented young people to its beautiful campus, and they, in turn, were instrumental in furthering Cranbrook Academy's ideal of integrated design wherever their careers led them.

High overhead its lights shall gleam,
Far, far below life's restless stream
Unceasingly shall flow;
For this was spun its lithe fine form,
To fear not war, nor time, nor storm,
For Fate had meant it so.
—Joseph P. Strauss,
The Mighty Task is Done

MIRACLE IN THE MIST

According to the authors of *The Builders: Marvels of Engineering* (The National Geographic Society, 1992): "Rising through the mist, the Golden Gate Bridge spans the entrance to San Francisco Bay in one 4,200-foot stride. Completed in 1937, it has the tallest towers of any bridge [750 feet]; trusses beneath the roadway stiffen the deck." The same source explains the four elements of a modern suspension bridge: its roadway, or deck, which usually stretches over the main span and the two side spans; towers at both ends of the main span; cables slung over the tops of the towers; and solid anchorages, normally at the ends of the side spans. Vertical supports called hangers, or suspenders, carry the deck weight and its live load up to the cables. This masterpiece of civil engineering resembles a great spiderweb flung across the majestic bay and is one of the most widely recognized symbols of the West. Architect Irving F. Morrow opted for an Art Deco form and chose the distinctive paint colour, known as "international orange," for its aesthetic appeal within the bay setting. Its namesake Golden Gate Park, with more than a thousand acres of woods and lakes, extends from the Pacific shore to the center of the city. It has miles of bridle paths, picnic and hiking areas, and four museums, as well as a public beach that runs along the western side of the city as far as Lake Merced.

AT A GLANCE: THE GOLDEN GATE BRIDGE

- The Golden Gate Strait was given its name by explorer John C. Fremont in the 1840s for its resemblance to Istanbul, Turkey's, natural harbor, the Golden Horn.
- With a span of 4,200 feet, the six-lane bridge was the world's longest for more than a quarter century, from its opening in May 1937 until 1964, when it was surpassed by New York City's Verrazano Narrows Bridge.
- Steel for the bridge was manufactured in five plants on the East Coast and shipped via the Panama Canal to San Francisco.

"This is an engineering victory of the first order—another great achievement of American resourcefulness, American skill and determination.
—President Franklin D. Roosevelt

AT A GLANCE: HOOVER DAM

- The Hoover Dam is 727 feet high, 1,244 feet long, and 660 feet thick at the base. Weighing more than 6.6 million tons, it is constructed of enough concrete to pave a highway from New York City to San Francisco.

- Strong enough to withstand water pressure of up to 45,000 pounds per square foot at its base, the dam contains Lake Mead, a 247-square-mile, 500-foot-deep reservoir with sufficient capacity to store the entire average flow of the Colorado River for a two-year period. This is enough water to cover the state of Pennsylvania to a depth of one foot.

- The dam is an arch-gravity structure; water is carried to the turbines both by the action of the horizontal arches and by gravity. The $165-million construction cost has since been paid, with interest, by sale of hydroelectric power.

THE GRAND DAM

Harnessing great rivers to produce hydroelectric power began in the United States in 1911, when the 280-foot-high Theodore Roosevelt Dam, a masonry-arch dam, opened in Arizona. It was not until 1936 that the enormous Hoover (formerly Boulder) Dam began operation after years of construction under the auspices of John Lucian Savage, chief design engineer for the U.S. Bureau of Reclamation. Its location on the Arizona-Nevada border made working conditions challenging, with high winds and temperatures that soared well over 100 degrees, but the Colorado River was diverted through four tunnels with the use of temporary cofferdams and the site was pumped dry for the excavation. Working twenty-four hours a day, the crews swung the first of more than 400,000 buckets of concrete into position for pouring into the wooden forms in June 1933. What was to be then the world's largest concrete dam—nearly a quarter of a mile long and more than the equivalent of seventy stories tall—took another three years of round-the-clock labor to complete.

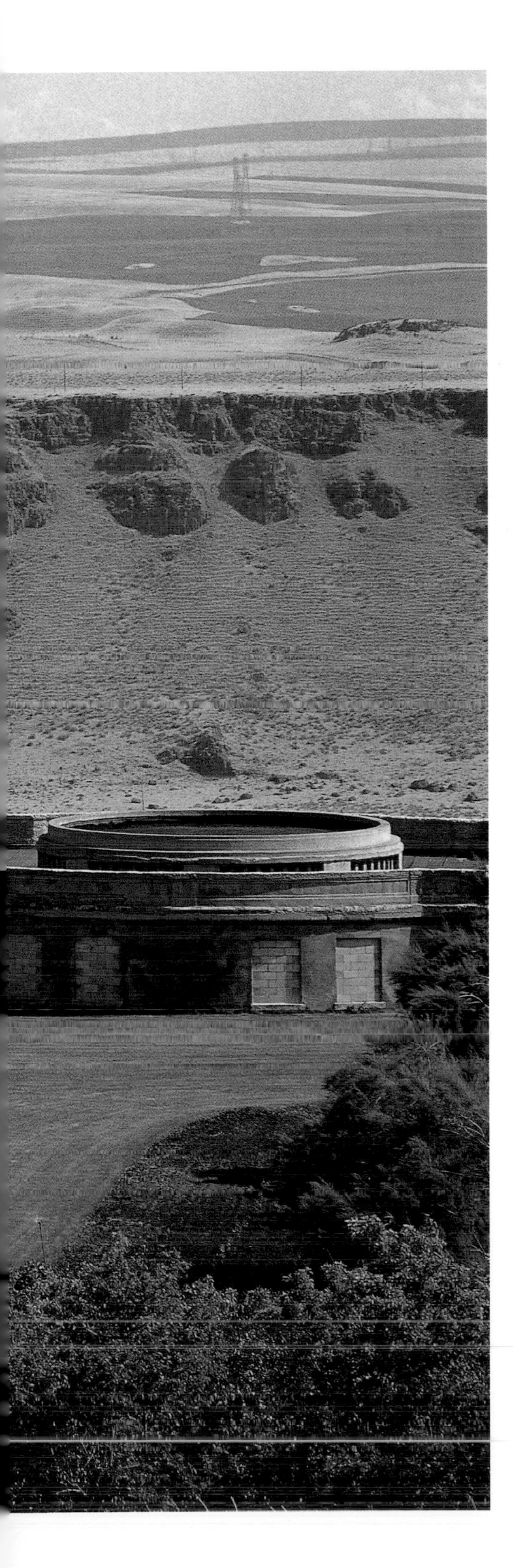

AT A GLANCE: MARYHILL MUSEUM OF ART

- Built by wealthy businessman, philanthropist, and Quaker pacifist Sam Hill, Maryhill Museum is built on land originally intended for an agricultural community.

- Hill was extremely well connected and had befriended Queen Marie of Romania by assisting her country after World War I. She dedicated the museum in 1926, bringing with her an array of opulent and exotic gifts.

- Hill died in 1931 before the museum's completion. The San Francisco sugar heiress Alma Spreckels oversaw and financed the museum's completion, and donated part of her own art collection. It opened in 1940 on Hill's birthday, May 13.

"There's a dream built into this place."
—Queen Marie of Romania

WHAT DREAMS MAY COME

This handsome institution, originally designed as a residence, stands in solitary splendor above the slopes of the Columbia River Gorge in Goldendale, Washington. Architects Hornblower and Marshall designed the building in 1914: its construction is of poured concrete on a steel I-beam frame—an early use of these materials in the United States.

Samuel Hill was a devoted art collector, and one of his first acquisitions was a number of Rodin sculptures. Through his friendship with Queen Marie of Romania, whose country he had helped with substantial funds after World War I, Hill received gifts including Russian icons, Fabergé objects, a coronation gown, crown jewels, and elegant furnishings. After Hill's death in 1931, San Francisco heiress Alma Spreckels was instrumental in bringing the museum's art collection to new levels and seeing Maryhill opened to the public.

"Fallingwater is Wright's greatest essay in horizontal space; it is his most powerful piece of structural drama; it is his most sublime integration of man and nature."

—Paul Goldberger,
The New York Times

AT A GLANCE: FALLINGWATER

- Fallingwater was created in 1936 for the Pittsburgh retail magnate Edgar J. Kaufmann, who became a close friend and patron of Frank Lloyd Wright.

- Critical acclaim for Wright's masterpiece of residential design helped confirm his status as one of the world's most prominent and innovative twentieth-century architects.

- In 1999 the Western Pennsylvania Conservancy was granted $901,000 by the Save America's Treasures grants program to strengthen the structure, which has been weakened over the decades by extremes of frost and thaw.

"There in a beautiful forest was a solid, high rock ledge rising beside a waterfall, and the natural thing seemed to be to cantilever the house from that rock bank over the falling water..."

—Frank Lloyd Wright

CONCRETE CASCADE

This renowned house is the fullest realization of Wright's lifelong ideal of a dwelling completely at one with its natural setting. Constructed on three levels primarily of reinforced concrete, sandstone, and glass, with its soaring cantilevered balconies anchored in solid rock, the house appears to float above the waterfall in its secluded wooded glen in the western Pennsylvania Highlands.

The planes of the house are held together by rough sandstone walls of varying thickness, quarried nearby and laid up in alternating courses. The southern exposure, facing the view of the stream, is walled primarily in glass. A particularly arresting feature is the multistoried shaft of mitered glass, stone, and steel that commands this view.

Most of the house's floor space is devoted to the massive, stone-flagged living room and the terraces and canopy-slabs that soar out in four directions. The three bedrooms, kitchen, and utility areas take up only a small proportion of the structure. In 1939 a guest house, with garage and servants' quarters, was added to the complex on a slope above the main house. It is reached by a winding, covered walkway that makes ingenious use of curved and geometric concrete forms. Similar forms encircle some of the trees in the garden, linking house and grounds like graceful ribbons.

Mr. Kaufmann, Sr., and the architect were brought together by Edgar J. Kaufmann, Jr., who had been one of Wright's apprentices at Taliesin. Later, he wrote the book *Fallingwater*, in which he stated that "My father was no monarch and his house was not conceived as a public monument." The fact that it became one did not detract from its original function as a much-loved family home.

AT A GLANCE: JOHNSON WAX BUILDING

- Frank Lloyd Wright's budget for design and construction of the S.C. Johnson and Son Administration Building was $200,000, a huge sum in the Depression years of the mid-1930s. Typically, though, Wright's vision far exceeded the budget, and the building eventually cost nearly $3 million.

- Johnson, a friend and admirer of the architect, gave him carte blanche over the design brief. Wright's creativity soared to new and extraordinary heights, expressed particularly in the half-acre Great Workroom with its delicate mushroom-shaped columns, top-lighted by streamlined glass tubing and skylights, and furnished with his own creations.

THE GRAMMAR OF SIMPLICITY

The intensely creative period of the 1930s resulted in one of Wright's best-known complexes—a milestone in commercial architecture. He undertook the commission for Herbert F. Johnson, who was president of the Johnson Wax Company. The businessman admired Wright's work and had become a personal friend. (The Research Tower, at left below, was added in 1944.) The Racine, Wisconsin, site suggested a self-contained, streamlined environment, and the sleek Administration Building was lighted by skylights and a clerestory band below the cornice.

"An inspiring a place to work in as any cathedral was in which to worship"
—Frank Lloyd Wright

The main building supports were dendriform (mushroom-shaped) columns, slender at the base and increasingly thicker as they rose toward the ceiling to become petal-shaped. The columns were made of hollow reinforced concrete, and window glazing was replaced by Pyrex tubing throughout the building. As it turned out, the Pyrex tubing of the skylights and covered walkways was not watertight, an ongoing problem that was finally solved by building a conventional skylit roof over the original one. (Wright airily dismissed the problem as a minor one—like the prohibitive cost overrun for the building itself. Fortunately, Mr. Johnson had a lot of money.) The architect also designed the clean-lined, contemporary furnishings for the building, including steel-and-wood desks that harmonized with the soft rust-colored interiors. The S.C. Johnson & Son Administrative Building opened in 1939 to instant acclaim and has since been designated for preservation by the AIA.

Above: *The reception area of the advertising department in the Johnson Research Tower features a domed ceiling of Pyrex tubing patterned with exterior circles.*

AT A GLANCE: THE FARNSWORTH HOUSE

- Designed by Ludwig Mies van der Rohe as a vacation retreat for distinguished Chicago physician Dr. Edith Farnsworth, the Farnsworth House is his only residential commission in the United States. Many of its features echo Mies's revolutionary design for the bold, planar Barcelona Pavilion (1929).

- Perfection in every detail drove construction costs through the roof; Dr. Farnsworth was invoiced $73,000 for the house—an enormous figure for the time (1946–51).

- The guiding principle behind van der Rohe's uncompromising aesthetic, dubbed the "International Style," was "driving to the essence of things." His stark, minimalist approach was both popular and controversial among critics and the public.

"Less is more."
—Ludwig Mies van der Rohe

MIESIAN MODERNISM

Architectural historian Joseph Giovanni has called Ludwig Mies van der Rohe's Farnsworth House in Plano, Illinois, "sublime...taut and tense because no parts are distant from their defining moments at the corners." Indeed, this essay in Miesian Modernism is virtually flawless in plan and execution, appearing to float above the ground in its wooded setting. The stark but lustrous minimalism that the great German architect had espoused, with Walter Gropius, at the Bauhaus founded in Dessau in 1919 had a profound impact upon American architecture when both men emigrated to the United States during the 1930s. In fact, the influential Museum of Modern Art in New York City has staged no fewer than nine exhibitions devoted to Mies's work since World War II.

THE LIGHT FANTASTIC

Mies's influence upon architect Philip C. Johnson is apparent in "The Glass House" that Johnson designed and built as his own residence in New Canaan, Connecticut (1946–49). This milestone in Modernism is entirely transparent except for a cluster of movable shades, and rises from a brick podium surrounding a brick chimney that penetrates the flat plane of the roof. The living space—32 x 56 feet—comprises dining, sitting, and sleeping areas along with a kitchen counter and the bathroom, within the brick core.

Johnson was one of the first Americans to study modern European architecture and to bring it to the attention of Americans as a curator of New York City's Museum of Modern Art. With architectural historian Henry-Russell Hitchcock (1903–87), he was coauthor of the seminal 1932 book *The International Style: Architecture Since 1922.*

> *"Why not take out the landscaping, the retaining walls, the colonnades? The building would be just as useful and much cheaper. True, an architect leads a hard life—for an artist."*
>
> —Philip Johnson

AT A GLANCE: THE GLASS HOUSE

- The Glass House was Philip Johnson's 1949 master's thesis project. The basic concept was derived from that of his mentor, Ludwig Mies van der Rohe.
- The walls of the structure are constructed entirely of glass, with movable translucent shades that can be positioned to provide a modicum of privacy.
- Philip Johnson coined the term "International Style" in 1932 when coauthoring a book for an exhibition at the Museum of Modern Art, New York, of which he was Director of the Department of Architecture.

AT A GLANCE: BETH SHOLOM SYNAGOGUE

- Rabbi Mortimer J. Cohen, who worked alongside architect Frank Lloyd Wright, envisioned the temple as a "mountain of light" symbolic of Israel's Mount Sinai, where Moses is believed to have received the Ten Commandments.
- A 160-ton steel tripod supports the thousands of panes of glass that comprise the building's 100-foot-high roof.
- The synagogue is one of seventeen structures designated by the American Institute as examples of Wright's outstanding contribution to the nation's culture.
- Frank Lloyd Wright died just five months before the dedication of the temple, which took place in September 1959.

I wanted to create the kind of building in which people, on entering it, will feel as if they were resting in the hands of God."

—Frank Lloyd Wright

TEMPLE OF LIGHT

One of Frank Lloyd Wright's major essays in architecture is this unique, transcendent temple commissioned in 1954 by the congregation of Beth Sholom, in Elkins Park, Pennsylvania, under the leadership of Rabbi Mortimer Cohen. Inspired by the rabbi's conception of the building as "a mountain of light, a moving Sinai," Wright worked closely with him to design this pyramidal structure of aluminum, steel, glass, and fiberglass, which rises from its hexagonal concrete base on a tripod formed by steel-and-concrete uprights. A cantilevered canopy (opposite) shelters the main entrance and overlooks a reflecting pool.

Inside, the main sanctuary is reached by two shallow, curving flights of stairs that open onto a worship space that can accommodate a thousand or more, seated at varying heights and levels. This interior is entirely free of columns or pillars, as the superstructure is supported by the concrete tripod. The sanctuary slopes gently toward the beautiful Ark (pictured at left), its primary focus. Daylight is filtered through the magnificent translucent pyramid overhead and changes through the course of the day from silver to gold. At night, the temple radiates light that can be seen from afar.

Below the main building are a chapel and two lounges for congregational gatherings, one of which is connected by a sheltered walkway to the adjacent school and social center. In keeping with the Judaic prohibition of "graven images" representing the Deity, ornaments to the building, including a triangular stained-glass panel overhanging the sanctuary (seen at left) and a menorah motif that recurs throughout the temple, are abstract symbols of this ancient faith.

"Here is a crucial opportunity to open the eyes not of Marin County alone, but of the entire country, to what officials gathering together might themselves do to broaden and beautify human lives."

—Frank Lloyd Wright

AT A GLANCE: MARIN COUNTY CIVIC CENTER

- The Marin County Civic Center was Frank Lloyd Wright's 770th commission, and was completed by his firm, Taliesin Architects, in 1969, ten years after Wright's death.
- Spanning three hills, the building's turquoise roofs are designed to complement the colors of the California sky.
- The complex's construction materials include steel framing, cement stucco for the arches, terrazzo for walkways and stairs, and sheet rock for partitions.
- The 172-foot spire and 80-foot-wide dome are inspired by the Oriental influences that informed Wright's design, as are the gold spheres adorning its exterior.

INTO THE FUTURE

Frank Lloyd Wright's futuristic Marin County Civic Center, in San Rafael, California, was designed two years before his death and completed afterward by Taliesin Architects Ltd. and the San Francisco-based architect Aaron Green. The center comprises a nearly circular post office of blacks and forms—the first building on the site (1962) and Wright's only commission from the federal government. The Administration Building and parallel Hall of Justice (1970) are multilevel arcaded buildings with barrel-vaulted concrete rooflines. Plastic skylights tinted blue illuminate the rows of offices within, which line a central well. The Administration Building features an atrium with balconies overlooking an indoor garden–an expression of Wright's career-long desire to "bring the outside in" by means of his designs.

The base of both buildings is concrete, cast in place: the arcaded walls above are of steel-framed stucco. The arcades become progressively smaller on each floor of the buildings, which creates a rhythmic horizontal line that converges upon the domed roof of the library. Natural light floods the complex from the glass walls that extend nearly the length of each floor, recessed behind the arcades in the sand-colored walls.

Ornamental metalwork recurs as a theme throughout the complex. The largest windows have grilles of steel piping painted terra-cotta red. Aluminum gates are formed of bent piping, and metal spheres line the lower edges of the overhanging roof. Geometric forms in aluminum appear in the balconies formed by the arcades. These motifs are mirrored in the interior designs and detailing throughout.

Many of the civic center's features were first envisioned in the 12-foot-square model of Broadacre City, built by Wright and members of the Taliesin Fellowship in 1934. Here, the visionary architect showed his Utopian ideas on urban planning appropriate to the American landscape and way of life. He allocated an acre of land to each citizen, and showed how cohesive communities could be created in natural settings closely linked by roadways and free of the noise, crowding, and pollution of the traditional city. However, the ideals he first put forward in *The Disappearing City* (1932) remained largely unrealized except in such isolated examples as the Marin County Civic Center.

***Opposite:** The ornamental aluminum pylon designed to serve as a dual-purpose ventilation tower and radio antenna on the Marin County Civic Center's Administration Building.*

> *"What intrigues me most is to imagine archaeologists five thousand years from now digging in New Haven... and finding this huge dinosaur-like skeleton. What kind of history will they reconstruct about what formidable creatures Yale men were in the mid-twentieth century?"*
>
> —Eero Saarinen

THE YALE WHALE

One of the nation's most distinguished collegiate hockey facilities, this unusual arena has commanded attention on the corner of Prospect and Sachem Streets, near the heart of the Yale campus, since the late 1950s. It has been speculated that Eero Saarinen's freeform design reflected the grace involved in skating. The rink seats 3,486 spectators and is made of con-

crete, with an aluminum roof supported by cables. The ceiling soars to a height of 76 feet at its zenith. In 1991, both the rink surface and its ice-making system were renovated at a cost of $1.5 million—equal to the original cost of construction. The playing surface, 200 feet long and 85 feet wide, is considered among the best in the country, and Yale's women's hockey team has been featured here since 1977.

AT A GLANCE: INGALLS HOCKEY ARENA

- Named for two captains of the Yale University Hockey team, David S. Ingalls and his son, the rink's hump-backed roof and 300-foot "spine" have earned it the nickname "the Yale Whale."
- Designed by Eero Saarinen, the structure's construction cost was $1.5 million, twice its original budget.

AT A GLANCE: O'HARE INTERNATIONAL AIRPORT

- Originally named Orchard Field, the airport's three-letter abbreviation, used on baggage and information displays, remains ORD.
- The airport was renamed for Lieutenant Commander Edward "Butch" O'Hare, whose outstanding courage during World War II saved the USS *Lexington*, a mission described by President Franklin D. Roosevelt as "one of the most daring, if not the most daring, single action in the history of combat aviation."
- In 1962, Chicago's Midway Airport transferred scheduled flights to O'Hare, increasing its annual passenger traffic to 10 million and making it the world's busiest airport. In 1999, more than 70 million travelers passed through O'Hare.

THE SKY'S THE LIMIT

More than 900,000 flights took off and landed at Chicago's O'Hare International Airport in 2001, reclaiming its title as the world's busiest airport. Since 1945, when Orchard Field, location of the Douglas aircraft assembly plant, was chosen for its location, significant expansion has occurred. Today's complex occupies nearly 7,700 acres, accommodating around 55,000 employees plus passenger traffic. Four terminals and 172 aircraft gates are linked by a warren of walkways, one housing "The Sky's the Limit," Michael Hayden's world-record-breaking kinetic neon sculpture, illuminating the 744-foot tunnel under Terminal One. Pioneering design includes the first airplane taxiway to span a public roadway, and fingerprint-recognition hardware.

Left: The International Terminal, which opened in 1993, was designed by a team including Chicago architect Ralph Johnson.

> *"This is an extraordinary airport...and it could be classed as one of the wonders of the modern world."*
>
> President John F. Kennedy

House

"This will be to Seattle what the Eiffel Tower is to Paris. The Space Needle will be the great symbol of a great city."
—Edward E. Carlson

AT A GLANCE: SEATTLE SPACE NEEDLE

- Built by architect John Graham, the tower's construction is fortified against seismic and meteorological activity. Its concrete foundation, 30 feet deep by 120 feet square, weighs more than the needle itself, ensuring that the structure's center of gravity is close to the ground.

- New computerized elevators move at the same speed as a raindrop falls, three times faster than snowfall. When descending during a flurry, the flakes appear to move upward!

HERE COMES THE TWENTY-FIRST CENTURY!

Seattle is just as proud of its unique Space Needle today as it was in 1962, when what would become the Emerald City's best-known symbol opened for the World's Fair. Its futuristic design, reflecting the fair's theme of the twenty-first century, was initially sketched on a cafe placemat by hotel magnate Edward E. Carlson, whose main inspiration was Germany's Stuttgart Tower. Technically advanced, the building is designed to withstand earthquake activity and winds of up to 200 m.p.h. Renovations made in the spring of 2000 include the addition of a glass-enclosed Pavilion that spirals around the base of the 605-foot tower and improvements at every level of this "vertical village," including the Observation Deck. Here, one can obtain a wide view of beautiful Puget Sound, an arm of the sea that has made Seattle a great port despite its relative distance from the Pacific Ocean. The interior of the Observation Deck features colorful displays of Space Needle history and trivia, and the revolving restaurant one level below is a popular venue for civic and private gatherings of all kinds.

"What had doomed the [original] glass and aluminum design from the beginning was the word "modernistic." To the Congressional mind, untutored in the recondite process of modern art, the word suggests such radical images as Pablo Picasso, one-eyed women, and melting watches."

—New York Times, July 17, 1955

THE SHOCK OF THE NEW

As built, Skidmore, Owings and Merrill's cadet chapel for the United States Air Force Academy in Colorado Springs has been described as "at once old and new, physical and spiritual, solid and soaring, of the earth and of outer space." So controversial was the chapel's original accordion-shaped design by SOM's Walter A. Netsch, Jr., that, in 1955, the House of Representatives refused funding for its construction and, quite unexpectedly, struck funds for other Air Force Projects. Netsch was given paid leave to recover and rework the design, and toured Europe both to rest and rethink his plans. Today's two-tier structure, reminiscent of a phalanx of jets aboard a carrier, was in fact inspired by the thirteenth-century Sainte-Chapelle in Paris. There are seventeen metal spires on the second tier, soaring to a height of more than 150 feet—they are in harmony with the backdrop of the Rocky Mountains and symbolize the spiritual aspect of the cadet's life, as expressed in "The Air Force Hymn": "Aloft in solitudes of space/Uphold them with your saving grace." The Cadet Chapel was envisioned as the crowning architectural feature of the campus and was under construction for four years, from August 1959 to the summer of 1963, under the auspices of contractor Robert E. McKee of Santa Fe, New Mexico.

AT A GLANCE: U.S.A.F. ACADEMY CADET CHAPEL

- The contract for construction of the chapel was put out to tender in 1954, when the academy's Project Office invited 260 architectural firms to compete for it.
- The chapel houses a number of separate spaces that are dedicated to a variety of faith communities.

"Passion for our work, our clients, our world."

—Bill Valentine, President, HOK Group, Inc.

CIRCLES OF FAITH

The graceful design of this circular chapel, with its tiers of parabolic arches, recalls the symbolism of the circle as an emblem of eternity, as seen in Christianity in the form of the Advent wreath and conjoined rings representing the Trinity. Crowning the edifice is the cross, the religion's principal icon. Architect Gyo Obata studied with Eliel Saarinen at Michigan's Cranbrook Academy of Art, and his mastery of integrated design principles is clear in this and other contemporary buildings.

AT A GLANCE: PRIORY CHAPEL, ST. LOUIS ABBEY

- In 1955 three Benedictine monks from England's Ampleforth Abbey established a monastery on the 150-acre site, 15 miles to the west of St Louis. Their vision was of a "living" building whose structure reflected contemporary culture and gave its congregation a strong sense of participation.
- The chapel was designed and built in 1962 by Gyo Obata, one of the founders of the Hellmuth Obata and Kassabaum group. Obata also designed the highly acclaimed National Air and Space Museum (1975) in Washington, DC.
- The building's three circular tiers of parabolic arches encircle a skylight that illuminates the altar below.

__Right:__ Each base of the 630-foot arch—the nation's tallest monument—is a powerful triangle with a solid filling of concrete encasing highly stressed steel rods carried deep into the foundations.

"Neither an obelisk nor a rectangular box nor a dome seemed right on this site or for this purpose. But here, at the edge of the Mississippi River, a great arch seemed right."

—Eero Saarinen

A TRIUMPHAL ARCH

Finnish-American architect Eero Saarinen won the design competition for the Jefferson National Expansion Memorial National Historic Site from a field of 171 entrants in 1948, thirteen years after President Franklin D. Roosevelt established the monument as a tribute to Thomas Jefferson and the countless explorers and pioneers who pushed the nation's boundaries west. St. Louis city fathers were instrumental in having the memorial approved because of the major role played by the Missouri city as a jumping-off place for those who crossed the Mississippi to settle previously unknown territory carved from the Louisiana Purchase of 1803.

A decade in the planning, Saarinen's revolutionary arch benefited from the input of project engineers led by John Dinkeloo, who had collaborated with Saarinen to implement the plan based on a single hollow, curving tube. Only special building materials and deep foundations could stabilize the form that would frame much of downtown St. Louis.

Stainless steel was chosen for its tensile strength, beauty, and resistance to corrosion. The Pittsburgh-Des Moines Steel Company fabricated the sections for the arch from 886 tons of the material—more stainless steel than had been used on any other single construction project, according to *The Builders: Marvels of Engineering* (The National Geographic Society, 1992). According to this authoritative work: "The arch features a strong, stressed-skin design. A cross-section of one of the legs reveals an equilateral triangle; each of the triangle's three sides is built from two walls of steel plate. High-strength steel bolts connect the two plates. Concrete, bolstered by steel tensioning rods, fills the space between the plates. By tightening the bolts and rods, the steel skin was stretched tight."

Entrance ramps at the bases of the arch give access to the underground visitor center and the Museum of Westward Expansion, completed in 1976. More recently, a large pool was centered at the subterranean core of the site. Most of the area below ground is occupied by the museum. Many of Saarinen's fellow architects believe that the Gateway Arch represents the summit of his career. In the words of the esteemed architect Cesar Pelli, the design was "a perfect combination of a free gesture with a romantic view of modern technology."

AT A GLANCE: ST. LOUIS GATEWAY ARCH

- Eero Saarinen won the 1947 competition to design a monument for the Jefferson National Expansion Memorial Park, to celebrate westward expansion since the Louisiana Purchase. Constructed between 1961 and 1965, it won the Institute of American Architects 25 Year Award in 1990.

- The space-age structure's design dates back to the seventeenth century. The catenary curve described by the arch's structure is based upon that resulting from hanging a chain upside-down from two points.

- At 630 feet, the arch is the nation's tallest monument. The distance between the two bases that carry its entire weight is the same as the building's height.

Left. *The arch's interior was designed to carry space-age capsules bearing five passengers each to the observation room, high above the city of St. Louis.*

Overleaf: *This unique monument is the zenith of the arch as used in architecture since ancient times.*

FIRSTAR

AT A GLANCE:
THE EPCOT DISCOVERY CENTER

- EPCOT is an acronym for Experimental Prototype Community of Tomorrow, designed by Walt Disney as "a showcase to the world for the ingenuity and imagination of American free enterprise."

- Walt Disney purchased more than 40 square miles of Florida swampland—twice the area of Manhattan—to create a real, working city—his own personal utopia.

- Spaceship Earth is one of the main attractions at Disney World®. The 180-foot geodesic dome encases an inner sphere in which the ride is housed. It weighs over 15 million pounds and took twenty-six months to build.

"It will never cease to be a living blueprint of the future, where people actually live a life they can't find anywhere else in the world."
—Walt Disney

"I would like to be part of building a model community, a City of Tomorrow, you might say, because I don't believe in going out to this extreme blue-sky stuff that some architects do. I believe that people still want to live like human beings."
—Walt Disney

FUTURE PERFECT

Walt Disney's initial vision of the Experimental Prototype Community of Tomorrow (EPCOT) generated intense excitement when it opened 15 miles south of Orlando, Florida. Accessed by a monorail loop from Disney World®, by far the nation's largest theme park, the site suggests a permanent world's fair built, as Disney expressed it, to showcase "the ingenuity and imagination of American free enterprise." The dazzling geosphere that houses Spaceship Earth towers 180 feet above the park, enclosing a 16-minute ride that explores the history of communication through Audio-Animatronic scenes of great vividness and accuracy. Spaceship Earth, composed of an aluminum compound known as alucabond, is actually two spheres, one inside the other, with the outer shell housing the inner core and ride system. This geodesic dome weighs more than 15 million pounds and is supported by six long legs that were sunk more than 100 feet into the ground.

AT A GLANCE: REUNION TOWER

- Constructed in 1978 as part of the Hyatt Regency Hotel, the fifty-story tower is one of Dallas's most prominent and well-known landmarks.

- The sphere sits atop a poured-concrete shaft and houses an observation deck, a restaurant, and a cocktail bar. The two upper levels rotate once every 55 minutes.

- The illuminations comprise 260 lights supported on a geodesic dome formed of aluminum struts. This architectural form, first designed by Buckminster Fuller, is identical to that of Spaceship Earth, and is the strongest and lightest structural design known to man.

"When I'm working on a problem, I never think about beauty. I think only how to solve the problem. But when I have finished, if the solution is not beautiful, I know it is wrong."
—Buckminster Fuller

GEOMETRY OF MIRACLES

Reunion Tower and the Hyatt Regency of Dallas were designed by Welton Becket & Associates of Los Angeles, California, and built in 1978. The shaft of the 560-foot-tall tower is made of poured-in-place concrete and features four concrete cylinders. The geodesic dome, with its signature sparkling lights that illuminate downtown Dallas's night sky, is formed with aluminum struts covered with 260 lights that flash to different patterns for a special light show at intervals during the evening. Both the full-service restaurant Antares and The Dome, an elegant cocktail lounge, are housed on a revolving floor that offers spectacular views of the Dallas skyline and the surrounding area. Reunion Tower is at this writing the city's fifteenth-tallest building.

AT A GLANCE: MARINA CITY

- Bauhaus-trained Bertram Goldberg's unusual design for Chicago's $36-million Marina City expressed nearly thirty years of architectural progress. The two cylindrical towers were, at the time of their construction, the tallest concrete structures in the world, their aerodynamic shape a direct solution to the "windy city" site.

- The building also broke the record for the tallest-ever residential complex, with the upper two-thirds of the sixty stories housing 450 apartments, arranged in radial segments around the central axis. The "city within a city" also contains a wealth of other facilities, both commercial and leisure.

- The towers' nickname of "corncob," inspired by the pattern on their surface, describes their design quite accurately. A central core, containing services and utilities, bears 70 percent of each structure's weight; the post-and-beam cage that surrounds it supports the remaining 30 percent.

"More than in any other high-rise apartments, in Marina City one has the feeling of having the whole city at one's feet."
—Wim de Wit

TOWERS OF STRENGTH

Chicago's skyline was still dominated by the Miesian aesthetic when architect Bertram Goldberg designed his radically different Marina City complex downtown, on the Chicago River. Completed in 1961, it is a distinctive multiuse facility that includes apartments, offices, and shops in its two circular towers. Not all critics were pleased by Marina City: Ada Louise Huxtable, for example, takes exception to various departures from the International Style, which she describes as "a twentieth-century vernacular style that is singularly suitable for the modern city's unique and overpowering scale.... Glass towers may reflect many of the defects of the society they serve, but their aesthetic mix of substance and reflection makes a magnificent street architecture." The reader will judge for himself.

"We have become aware of the almost alive quality which our structures achieve, and we seek the forms which give the most life to our structures."
—Bertram Goldberg

" Its soaring atrium was wildly successful and became the signature piece of our hotels around the world. It was immediately apparent that this design had a pronounced effect on the mood of our guests and attitude of our employees."

—Thomas J. Pritzker

AT A GLANCE: HYATT REGENCY HOTEL, ATLANTA

- The Hyatt Regency was John Portman's first hotel design, and its twenty-two-story atrium, revolving restaurant, and glass elevators enthralled and revolutionized the entire industry.
- The Pritzker family, owners of the hotel group, later created a prestigious award, sometimes called the "Nobel Prize of Architecture," carrying their name. The work of some of its laureates, including Philip Johnson, Ieoh Ming Pei, and Frank O. Gehry, can be found in these pages.

NEW HEIGHTS

Architect and developer John Portman had studied both Rockefeller Center and the Tivoli Gardens in Copenhagen before he designed this flagship Hyatt Regency Hotel for the Peachtree Center complex. According to architectural historian Paul Goldberger, the hotel's immense atrium made the facility "in effect an indoor plaza and a piece of theater second to none in American architecture of its time….His complexes are [distinguished] by considerable attention to social interaction through the provision of cafes, parklike alcoves, and ample retail space." Many features of the hotel's design were repeated frequently within the Hyatt group and were soon imitated in new hotels designed for the group's competitors, particularly the use of glass elevators overlooking an expansive atrium or courtyard.

"The building adds to the skyline not so much an object as a spectacle of changing light, an intensified comment on the qualities of the sky itself."
—Donlyn Lyndon

PEI IN THE SKY

I.M. Pei and Henry Cobb, his chief design partner, produced several impressive towers of reinforced concrete during the 1960s and '70s, all of which featured rhythmic façades of concrete with windows inset in a wafflelike grid. Kips Bay Plaza in New York City (1965) is one of the best examples. But for the John Hancock Tower on Copley Square in Boston (1975), the partners turned to glass sheathing, with startling results. In 1972, just before the tower was completed, its windows began to fall out! Eventually, they all had to be replaced: meanwhile, they were replaced with wooden panels, which suggested the prevalent witticism that the tower should be renamed the U.S. Plywood Building. However, when the John Hancock Tower opened with newly designed windows in 1975, the joke was on its critics. The base of the building reflected Henry Hobson Richardson's beautiful Trinity Church (see page 68) along its front and Henry Hardenbergh's handsome Copley Plaza Hotel (1912) along its side. Aesthetically, the tower takes the form of a parallelogram, with an indent above its short base that extends the full sixty stories of its height. In all, the surface includes some thirteen acres of glass. Like the initially controversial pyramidal glass addition Pei designed for the Louvre, Paris, in 1989, the Hancock Tower's radical design would prove to have popular appeal and become an asset in this venerable neighborhood instead of a liability.

AT A GLANCE: JOHN HANCOCK TOWER, BOSTON

- Situated close to historic Copley Square and traditional landmarks including the Boston Public Library and Trinity Church (page 68), I.M. Pei's futuristic 790-foot skyscraper was a focus of controversy from its conception.
- Constructed between 1972 and 1976, disaster struck when the two-ply windows started to fall from their frames. A huge reglazing project replaced more than 10,000 panes.

"It was as essential to us to expose the structure of this mammoth as it is to perceive the structure of the Eiffel Tower; for Chicago, honesty of structure has become a tradition."
—Bruce Graham

AT A GLANCE: JOHN HANCOCK CENTER, CHICAGO

- Towering 1,127 feet above Chicago, the John Hancock Center, designed by Bruce Graham of architects Skidmore, Owings and Merrill, is one of the nation's tallest buildings, competing with only the Sears and Amoco Towers and New York City's Empire State Building.
- Instantly recognizable for its criss-crossed surface, the structure comprises a tapered steel tube, its huge external beams and columns bracing the tower against the city's gales.
- Like Marina City (page 164), the John Hancock Center is a multiuse building, its 1.1 million square feet of space being used for commercial, leisure, and residential purposes.

BIG JOHN

Bruce Graham of Skidmore, Owings and Merrill, deeply influenced by Mies van der Rohe, was responsible for the design of this Chicago skyscraper, which was completed in 1969. At one hundred stories high, it forms a tall shaft that narrows gradually on all four sides as it rises. The engineering was supervised by Fazlur Kahn, who went on to use similar methods for the Sears Tower of 1974 (see page 171). The 94th-floor Observatory offers unparalleled views of Chicago and the surrounding area and is especially popular at sunset, appealing to Chicagoans and tourists alike. Architectural historian Paul Goldberger has written that "It proudly, almost arrogantly, displayed its structural reinforcements—huge X-braces cutting across the façade. It was a building of swagger, of enormous strength, although its shape made it a less than compatible neighbor on North Michigan Avenue. The tower seemed like a looming giant." It would soon be overtopped by SOM's Sears Tower.

Overleaf: *The John Hancock Center rises high above its neighbors on the Chicago skyline.*

AT A GLANCE: TRANSAMERICA PYRAMID

- At forty-eight stories and 853 feet, San Francisco's Transamerica Pyramid is the city's tallest building.
- Its distinctive shape serves two purposes; the tapered tower allows more sunlight to reach the street than does the traditional rectangular form, and offers a variety of office shapes and sizes, from just over 2,000 to more than 20,000 square feet.

"I left my heart in San Francisco."
—Tony Bennett
(words and music by
Douglas Cross and George Cory)

HALFWAY TO THE STARS

Architect William Pereira's unconventional pyramidal tower for Transamerica Corporation (1976) aroused considerable controversy when it first took shape in San Francisco. City planners rejected Transamerica's request to build a taller skyscraper in order to placate residents of Nob Hill, who feared for their highly prized views of the Bay. Based on an unbuilt project conceived during the 1960s for the American Broadcasting Company in New York City, the tower rises to a sharp narrow point more typical of the New York or Chicago tower than of San Francisco. However, as Paul Goldberger points out in *The Skyscraper,* "Transamerica has turned out to be less destructive to San Francisco than many other, less unusual, skyscrapers: its thin and eccentric shape in fact intrudes only slightly on the city's skyline. It is also one of the best examples of the skyscraper as image maker since [the] Woolworth [Building] (page 104)—the Transamerica Corporation uses the building as a symbol in its advertising and has made of it an internationally known icon."

Located in the financial district of San Francisco's downtown, the instantly recognizable profile of this elegantly shaped building can be seen from many parts of the city and its suburbs (see the view from Alamo Square in the photograph on pages 82–83). The external columns on either side of the tower serve both a functional and an aesthetic purpose, containing an elevator shaft on one wing and an emergency stair on the other.

> *"The technical man must not be lost in his own technology. Life is art, drama, music...and, most importantly, people."*
>
> —Fazlur Rahman Khan

AT A GLANCE: SEARS TOWER

- America's tallest building owes its strength to a bundle of nine reinforced tubes. Developed by engineer Fazlur Rahman Khan, this technology revolutionized tall-building design.
- Soaring 1,454 feet skyward—more than one-quarter mile—the 110-story building contains enough steel to make 50,000 automobiles, concrete to build an eight-lane, five-mile-long highway, and telephone wiring to span the world 1.75 times. The $150-million building weighs a half billion pounds (nearly one-quarter million tons).

ON A CLEAR DAY YOU CAN SEE FOREVER

The world's tallest building, Chicago's Sears Tower, was designed by Bruce Graham and Fazlur Khan of Skidmore, Owings and Merrill—the same team as for the nearby John Hancock Center (page 167)—and was completed in 1974. As many architectural historians have observed, the design was deeply influenced by Mies van der Rohe's axiom that "less is more," and true to its title as the champion high-rise, it bears the unmistakable imprint of the great German-American Modernist. Its structure is unusual—a series of square tubular towers of varying heights seemingly bundled together as they rise to a slender topmost tower crowned by a decisive finial. The design is both elegant and functional and has stood up handsomely when compared with what some consider the vagaries of some of the more recent developments in Postmodernism, which have been described by architectural writer Richard Lacayo as "whimsy, streetscapes modeled after the Magic Kingdom and office towers topped by medieval crenellations" ("Mies is More," *Time*, June 25, 2001).

"Suddenly I realized that architecture could have a deep social purpose. That was a revelation to me, and I knew it was something I wanted to do for the rest of my life."

—Cesar Pelli

AT A GLANCE: PACIFIC DESIGN CENTER

- With its glass membrane in varying shades of green and blue, Cesar Pelli's exuberant and ultramodern Pacific Design Center is nicknamed the "Blue Whale" by locals.
- The complex includes 130 showrooms displaying and selling more than 2,000 product lines of furniture, wall coverings, fabrics, lighting, floor coverings, and other designer goods.
- Born in Argentina, where he studied architecture as an undergraduate, Pelli earned a scholarship to study for a master's degree in architecture at the University of Illinois and has remained in the United States ever since.

THE BLUE WHALE

The versatile Cesar Pelli, a native of Argentina, has had an impressive career in international architecture, and in his adopted country as well, as seen on these two pages. Still growing, his Pacific Design Center complex opened in Los Angeles in September 1975 with the blue-glazed curtain-wall structure called Center Blue, which housed design offices and showrooms in a striking venue of 750,000 square feet. The beautifully landscaped 14-acre site gained a second building in 1988: Center Green, a square structure with truncated corners on a blue base, which provided an additional 450,000 square feet of space, almost half of which was converted to creative office space in 2001. The site plan calls for a third phase, Center Red. Meanwhile, the Pacific Design Center has become the West Coast's largest resource for architects and designers.

"Cities are our most important responsibility. They are the whole of which our buildings are the parts. Making a building one with its place has been a constant goal of architecture throughout the ages."

—Cesar Pelli

A POSTMODERN PHOENIX

Cesar Pelli and Associates designed this impressive commercial center (1988) in Minneapolis, Minnesota, which shows how the firm has moved from late Modernism into materials and forms that are more responsive to historic skyscrapers of the early twentieth century. Originally called the Norwest Tower, the building was rechristened with the merger of Norwest and Wells Fargo. A quality of what Frank Lloyd Wright described as "romanza" is apparent in this complex, with its pleasing, irregular outline and distinctive ornamental crown. Height is not the focal point, although it rises to fifty-seven stories—the city's second-tallest building—while First Bank Place stands fifty-three stories high. The design is solidly anchored at ground level, which is not the case with many of the stark skyscrapers of the International Style, which seem to improve in appearance the higher they go, since their bases often appear inadequate to support them—the "box on stilts" syndrome. The interior of the Wells Fargo Center also harks back to a more opulent style in commercial architecture, with a great paneled vault pierced by clerestory windows, a painted dome, a full-block indoor pedestrian promenade, and leaded-glass chandeliers. Pelli's Key Tower, built three years later in Cleveland, Ohio, bears many similarities to the Wells Fargo Center and closely resembles his first proposed design for this Minneapolis landmark.

AT A GLANCE: WELLS FARGO CENTER, MINNEAPOLIS

- Built to replace the Northwestern National Bank building, which burned down on Thanksgiving Day, 1982, Cesar Pelli's award-winning Wells Fargo Center was erected in 1988.
- With its cascading setbacks, the fifty-seven-story building pays tribute to New York City's Rockefeller Center. A key feature of postmodern architecture, the synthesis of historic and modern attributes is characteristic of Pelli's mature work.

AT A GLANCE:
THE CRYSTAL CATHEDRAL

- The Crystal Cathedral was founded by evangelists Reverend and Mrs. Robert Schuller and designed by Pritzker Laureate Philip Johnson in collaboration with John Burgee. It replaced a drive-in church whose capacity was 600 cars.
- Two 90-foot automatic doors give access to a sanctuary that seats nearly 3,000 people. The 185-foot chancel—made of Rosso Alicante marble quarried in Spain and finished in Italy—can accommodate 1,000 singers and instrumentalists.
- Well-wishers donated 500 dollars each for one of the 10,000 windows, and the entire construction cost of the 16.8-million-dollar building was paid for upon completion.

"And yet, what thrill can be as great as a design carried through, a building created in three dimensions, partaking of painting in color and detail, partaking of sculpture in shape and mass. A building for people, people other than oneself, who can rejoice together over the creation."

—Philip Johnson

CATHEDRAL OF LIGHT

Architects Philip C. Johnson and John Burgee, who were partners for twenty years, collaborated on the bold design of the Crystal Cathedral (1980) in Anaheim, California. Commissioned by the popular evangelists Reverend and Mrs. Robert Schuller, whose congregation had outgrown their previous house of worship, the structure comprises 10,000 windows of clear glass set into a metal grid that upholds the massive volumes of the building in a framework that seems as light as a spider's web. Springing still higher is the innovative tower that flanks the main church, with its slender, multilevel spires reminiscent of a medieval cathedral. Two massive contemporary pipe organs and the triangular loft that appears to float above the sanctuary contribute to the impressive interior of this neoclassical space, which seats 3,000 worshippers. Because broadcasting and liturgical music are prominent parts of the Schullers' ministry, the marble chancel that extends for almost 200 feet can accommodate up to 1,000 choristers and instrumentalists. The cathedral is a popular venue for celebrations of all the major Christian feasts, weddings, and lively pulpit exchanges with scripture scholars of international renown. Evangelist Billy Graham was instrumental in encouraging the Schullers to build the complex, which was paid in full by donations from thousands of individual contributors upon completion at a cost of $16.8 million.

Johnson's eminence as an architectural historian is apparent in his numerous designs. He has said of contemporary architecture, "I do not think we are in a great age of form innovation. The good architecture of this period no doubt has many features of Le Corbusier, Mies, and of other periods, because we are in a consolidating as well as a centrifugal period...The search is for expression now, rather than for function." During his association with John Burgee (1967–91), the two collaborated on several other notable structures, including the addition to the Boston Public Library (1973) and on Pennzoil Place in Houston, Texas (1976). These and an impressive portfolio of other buildings show Johnson's abiding concern with beautiful materials used in imaginative and daring ways. His own residence in Connecticut, the Glass House (1949), is featured on page 144.

"A graceful arc of green glass makes a sculptural statement that works in the wide-open context of the Wacker Drive river corridor; meanwhile, the building's other façade, which is sliced and notched, suits the grittier, more confined district of the Loop."

—Blair Kamin
Architecture critic, Chicago Tribune

REFLECTIONS

This impressive skyscraper by architects Kohn, Pederson, Fox in association with Perkins and Will is best viewed in its context—the area that begins at the fork of the Chicago River on Wolf Point. This is the heart of downtown Chicago, which begins a block west of Michigan Avenue and comprises an area five blocks wide and seven blocks long, defined by the elevated railroad (popularly known as the Loop) that was built to encircle it. Wacker Drive is the double-decked boulevard that forms one end of the Loop. The office tower at 333 was built between 1979 and 1983 of steel, glass, granite, and marble, at the apex of South Wacker Drive, Franklin Street, and Lake Street, and was immediately recognized as a landmark. Joyce Goldenstern, a volunteer docent with Chicago Architecture Foundation Tours, leads a walking tour through the area called "Fork of the River," in which she explains that "A theme of the tour might be 'layers': layers of history, from the fork as a trade, transportation and commercial center to a living and office-working center today; layers of geography, from river level to street level, to sky-walk level, each with its own perspective on the architecture of the area....I think this is the only tour that views 333 Wacker from both its street view and river view: good examples of contextualism both!"

The design of 333 Wacker Drive is especially remarkable for the contrast between the postmodern glass arc facing spacious Wacker Drive and the series of setbacks and notches facing the more constricted Loop, demonstrating the architects' careful consideration of the building's context. The architects also made clever use of the triangular lot by adapting the building to its site. As observed by architectural historian Paul Goldberger in *The Skyscraper* (Alfred A. Knopf, 1981): "[Some of the 1980s towers] do appear to accommodate themselves more directly to their architectural contexts. A number of glass towers designed by Kohn, Pederson, Fox are particularly noteworthy for the attention they pay to the massing, if not to the materials, of surrounding structures. Projects such as 333 Wacker Drive in Chicago and a series of schemes for the Bunker Hill area in Los Angeles are spirited and yet respectful." The distinctive reflecting curved façade of 333 Wacker Drive was portrayed in posters for the 1998 movie *The Truman Show* (Universal Studios) as a giant photomontage television screen.

Opposite: *The graceful arc of the curved façade of Kohn, Pederson, Fox's first skyscraper, which justifiably made the architects famous.*

AT A GLANCE: 333 WACKER DRIVE

- Hailed as Chicago's first postmodern skyscraper, the thirty-six-story 333 Wacker Drive office building is 487 feet tall and provides over 1 million square feet of office space.
- Designed by architects Kohn, Pederson, Fox Associates, the structure has won the American Institute of Architects' Honors Award (1984) and the Friends of Downtown Award for Best New Building Design (1986).
- The multilevel Wacker Drive, completed in 1926, is an advanced roadway whose octagonal columns supporting the upper level were a notable engineering innovation. The drive is flanked by fifty-seven high-rise buildings.

AT A GLANCE: HUMANA BUILDING

- Winner of an architectural competition launched by health benefits company Humana Inc., Michael Graves designed its twenty-seven-story headquarters in varying shades of stone. The exterior is mainly granite-slab, while the lobby is finished in colored marble: white, green, and beige from Italy; and black from France.

- The building's geometric planes and sharp curves bear no small similarity to those on the highly fashionable kitchenware of Italian designer Alessi; the creation of its iconic teapot in the same year as the Humana Building's completion helped make Graves's work internationally popular.

"The marble not yet carved can hold the form of every thought the greatest artist has."
—Michelangelo Buonarotti

MARBLE HALLS

Postmodern architect Michael Graves designed this striking building in Louisville, Kentucky (1985), for a site near the Ohio River, transitional between the lower traditional buildings of the old part of the city and the high-rise towers of downtown Louisville, including Mies van der Rohe's First National Bank Building. Several critics have observed that the Humana Building's façade, with its projecting terrace and conference room at the 26th-floor level, recall the Ohio River bridges and locks along one of the nation's foremost inland waterways. Others see allusions to Classicism translated from wood and stone into concrete and stone veneer. Still others applaud Graves's commitment to the creation of enclosed spaces that are designed for human occupation and habitation, as opposed to what Steven Kent Peterson has defined as the Miesian Modern space, which "often results in the creation of 'Anti-spaces,'" negating spatial character and definition. The general consensus is firmly that the Humana Building is an appropriate and distinctive building for its place and time.

THE SHAPE OF THINGS TO COME

Frank O. Gehry has said of his unusual commission for the Frederick R. Weisman Museum of Art at Minnesota's University of Minneapolis, "They told me not to build another brick lump." Clearly, the Deconstructivist designer complied with this mandate when he planned this bold, award-winning stainless-steel and brick museum. The sculptural façade commands views of the Mississippi River and the Minneapolis skyline, and the four-story structure has some 11,000 square feet of gallery space, a 120-seat auditorium, office and meeting/class rooms, and a museum store, among other amenities. Gifted photographers have studied the building from every angle and commented upon its integrity and the way it changes with the light of day, taking on at sunset all the blazing colors over the Mississippi below.

AT A GLANCE: WEISMAN ART MUSEUM

- Winner of the prestigious Progressive Architecture Design Award in 1991, Frank Gehry's gallery is more sculpture than a structure, its unique form perfectly expressing the building's function.
- An early prototype of another Gehry building that rocked the art world—Bilbao's Guggenheim Museum—the Weisman Art Museum's brushed-steel exterior has inspired similar projects worldwide, including Britain's Lowry Museum.
- Space-age engineering techniques and computer technology were used to create a design that maximizes the quality of light both inside and outside the building. Skylights illuminate the interior with natural light, while the polished surfaces reflect the location's beautiful skyscapes.

"They told me not to build another brick lump."

—Frank Gehry

AT A GLANCE: UNITED STATES HOLOCAUST MEMORIAL MUSEUM

- James Ingo Freed, of Pei Cobb Freed and Partners, and his team toured Europe visiting Holocaust sites for inspiration for this profoundly solemn memorial project.
- The brutal simplicity of the structure is designed to disturb the visitor, using such features as light and shadow within the interior spaces to generate an emotionally charged atmosphere.
- The hexagonal Hall of Remembrance, the visitor's final destination of the tour, is one example of the use of symbolism throughout the museum, representing both the 6 million Jews who died in the Holocaust and the Star of David.

"You can only try to recreate, through atmospheric effects, a devastating experience with deep emotional connotations for millions of people. The space inside the Holocaust Museum deals with dualities—dark and light, transparency and opacity, openness and constriction—to create a fundamental sense of disquiet."

—James Ingo Freed

NEVER FORGET

According to Jeff Goldberg's article on the Holocaust Museum, architect James Ingo Freed, of Pei Cobb Freed & Partners, visited a number of Holocaust sites, including camps and ghettos, to make referential drawings that resulted in the building's abstract forms, including the curved portal at the entrance, which are not designed to be understood intellectually, but "viscerally." As the architect says, "It must take you in its grip....There are no literal references to particular places or occurrences from the historic event. Instead, the architectural form is open-ended so the Museum becomes a resonator of memory." The building houses permanent and temporary exhibition spaces, a research library and archives, two theaters, an interactive computer learning center, classrooms, a memorial space, and areas for impromptu discussion. It has been widely acclaimed as a permanent living memorial to the millions who perished in the Holocaust.

SOL Y SOMBRA

Architect Antoine Predock, working mainly in the Southwest for more than thirty years, has become well known as a distinguished designer of performing arts centers and art museums, including the Spencer Theater for the Performing Arts in Alto, New Mexico, and the Tacoma Art Museum in Tacoma, Washington. Here at Tempe, Arizona, his genius for desert-oriented design is clearly apparent in the way that the Nelson Fine Arts Center melds itself in the university's urban/desert location. The auditorium and theater entry is accessed by piercing a circular brick arcade, which also serves as an aqueduct to deliver water to three fountains, one at the theater entrance. The gallery area is essentially a subterranean court that becomes progressively cooler as one moves through its underground spaces, circled by trellised walkways. The building won an AIA award in 1990. As one observer has remarked, "The center confronts the desert in a series of spaces that creates a procession from the open exterior to the intimate spaces of the interior."

"The Fine Arts Center...tells us, as eloquently as any building of the last few years, how it is possible for a piece of architecture to be deeply ingrained in the architectural traditions of a place, yet unlike anything we have seen before."

—Paul Goldberger,
New York Times

AT A GLANCE: NELSON FINE ARTS CENTER

- Antoine Predock's radical design for Arizona State University's Nelson Fine Arts Center pays tribute to Garcia Lorca's description of the desert's polarities—*"sol y sombra"* (sun and shadow). The complex's features meld with the colors and textures of its environment, creating a dramatic effect.

- Predock's influences include Frank Lloyd Wright and Louis Kahn, both of whom drew their primary inspiration from the site of construction and wider surroundings.

- The architect's multidisciplinary background—he studied painting with the Abstract Expressionist Elaine DeKooning and co-directed a contemporary dance project—made him an ideal choice for the project.

AT A GLANCE: FRED HARTMAN BRIDGE

- Constructed between 1992 and 1995, the Fred Hartman Bridge, spanning the Houston Ship Channel, was honored with the American Society of Civil Engineers' Outstanding Civil Engineering Award.
- The twin-decked cable-stay structure, spanning 1,250 feet, is longer than any other of Texas's estimated 50,000 bridges.

"Ah! The bridge of grace will bear your weight, brother."
—Charles Spurgeon

GIANT'S CAUSEWAY

This award-winning eight-lane, cable-stayed bridge spanning the Houston Ship Channel between Baytown and La Porte, Texas, is the world's largest suspension bridge of its kind. The double diamond towers supporting the fan-shaped cable configuration stand as tall as a forty-five-story building, and the longest of its 192 cables stretches 650 feet from the bridge to the towers. Both the pylons and the superstructure are of prestressed concrete. Designed by the engineering firms of Leonhardt, Andra and Partners and URS Greiner Woodward Clyde, the Baytown Bridge, as it is also called, carries Texas State Road 146 across the channel and replaces the Baytown-La Porte Tunnel, which was opened in 1953. The bridge has a capacity of 200,000 vehicles per day, as compared to the tunnel's capacity of 25,000 per day. It was built by Williams Brothers Construction between 1986 and 1995 at a cost of $100 million and utilizes more than 40 million pounds of steel and more than 3 million cubic feet of concrete. In 1996 the bridge received the Merit Bridge Award from the American Institute of Steel Construction.

GAZETTEER

ALABAMA

MOBILE

Fort Conde: reconstruction of the city's original French fort (1724)
Historic District: 59 buildings, mostly pre-Civil War

BIRMINGHAM

Sloss Furnaces: defunct pig iron plant, built 1881–82, now a National Historic Landmark and museum of industry
Civil Rights Institute: 1960s structure of epic scale and architecture

MOUNDVILLE

Moundville Archeological Park: preserves 26 prehistoric earthen mounds, the largest supporting a rebuilt Native American temple; it is estimated that 3,000 people occupied the area in the twelfth century

HUNTSVILLE

Twickenham Historic District: more than 65 antebellum structures

SELMA

Brown Chapel AME Church: organized by freed men after the Civil War, it is noted for its exterior Byzantine design; it was headquarters for the 1965 Voting Rights marches
Sturdivant Hall: erected in 1853, a beautiful plantation house

FLORENCE

Rosenbaum House: designed by Frank Lloyd Wright in 1939 for a college professor; typically Usonian in design

ALASKA

WRANGELL

Tlingit Tribal House of the Bear: reproduction of a community house, a large cedar building, that would have housed 50-100 people during the winter

CORDOVA

"Million Dollar Bridge": built in 1911 to span the Copper River at a cost of $1.5 million—an engineering feat of the time

KENNICOTT

More than 30 preserved buildings of a c. 1900 copper mining boomtown

JUNEAU

South Franklin Street Historic District: many buildings from the 1883–1939 gold mining era
Saint Nicholas Russian Orthodox Church: small, onion-domed structure built in 1893–4
Sentinel Island Lighthouse: originally constructed 1902, this art deco signal building was built 1935
Governor's Mansion: ornate structure of 1914
State Capitol: completed in 1931, the limestone and marble used in the four columns of the portico and in the lobby were quarried on Prince of Wales Island and in front of the building is a replica of the Liberty Bell

SITKA NATIONAL HISTORICAL PARK

Site of the *Tlingit Fort* and battlefield; Southeast Alaska totem poles; and the 1843 log *Russian Bishop's House*, one of three surviving examples of Russian colonial architecture in North America

SKAGWAY

Arctic Brotherhood Hall: built in 1899 with pedimented windows and a façade made of more than 20,000 small sticks of driftwood
Historic District: includes the 1900 Peniel Mission, 1898 log cabins, a 1903 saloon, and various stores

ANCHORAGE

4th Avenue Theatre: Art Deco style; first opened in 1947
Oscar Anderson House: one of the city's first houses, built in 1915 by a Swedish immigrant
Alaska Center for the Performing Arts: lobbies are decorated with Alaskan art, including 23 Native American masks
Kimball Building: on completion in 1915, one of the few multistory buildings in the city; a good example of an early commercial building

UNALASKA

Church of the Holy Ascension: Russian Orthodox church, with some portions dating from 1826

ARIZONA

TOMBSTONE

Crystal Palace Saloon: restored to its original appearance of 1879
Bird Cage Theater: notorious theater, saloon, and brothel, preserved with original fixtures from 1881
Tombstone Courthouse State Historic Park
O.K. Corral: scene of legendary gunfight involving the Earp brothers and "Doc" Holliday

CASA GRANDE RUINS NATIONAL MONUMENT

Ruins of the largest known Hohokam building, dated c.1320, perhaps used for astronomical observation

APACHE TRAIL

Roosevelt Dam: the highest masonry dam in the world, completed in 1911

PHOENIX

Arizona State Capitol Museum: 1899, the original territorial capitol building

GRAND CANYON NATIONAL PARK

Grand Canyon Village Historic District: many structures designed by Mary E. J. Colter, modeled after Native American themes; includes the Hopi House of 1905; Lookout Studio and Hermits Rest (1914); Phantom Ranch (1922); the Desert View Watchtower (1932); and Bright Angel Lodge (1935)

NAVAJO NATIONAL MONUMENT

Over 700 prehistoric sites; an Anasazi dwelling place of the thirteenth century; features ***Keet Seel***, a preserved cliff-palace of 155 rooms, its occupation dating from the tenth century

THE HOPI RESERVATION

Visits only with a guide and permission from the Cultural Preservation Office
First Mesa: contains the villages of Hano, Sichomovi, and Walpi
Second Mesa: the village of Shongopovi and the Hopi Cultural Center
Third Mesa: contains the village of Old Oraibi, inhabited since 1150, Hotevilla, and Bacabi

FLAGSTAFF

Riordan State Historic Park: a 40-room log mansion, built in 1904, with original furnishings
Wupatki National Monument: includes the ***Wupatki Ruin***, a pueblo c.1120; ***Wukoki***, a three-story pueblo; ***Citadel***, a two-story pueblo; ***Nalakihu Ruin***, a ten-room excavation; and ***Lomaki Ruin***, a pueblo dated c.1192

HOOVER DAM: *see* page 137

TUCSON

Mission San Xavier del Bac: *see* pages 28–31

TEMPE

Nelson Fine Arts Center: *see* page 181

ARKANSAS

HOT SPRINGS

Bathhouse Row: eight magnificent buildings, built between 1915 and 1962

LITTLE ROCK

Old State House Museum: the most impressive rooms are the two senate chambers, restored to their original grandeur

FORT SMITH

Fort Smith National Historic Site: remains of the original fort, Parker's courtroom, the basement jail and a set of gallows

VAN BUREN

Old Main Street: a stretch of more than seventy restored buildings that has been used in numerous Westerns

EUREKA SPRINGS

Thorncrown Chapel: the magnificent wooden structure rises 48 feet high; opened in 1980, it contains 425 windows and over 6,000 square feet of glass, atop 100 tons of native stone and colored flagstone

CALIFORNIA

CARMEL

Mission San Carlos Borromeo del Río Carmelo: restored 1797 mission

Torr House and Hawk Tower: 1919 home of the poet Robinson Jeffers, built with stones from all over the world, some from the Great Wall of China

SAN SIMEON

Hearst Castle: one of the most extravagant houses in the world

MONTEREY

The Old Custom House: oldest public building in California, in service from 1820s

First Brick House in California: built 1846 by a settler with homemade bricks of fired clay

Presidio: one of the most historically significant sites in California, a military-fort site through the Spanish, Mexican, and American eras

SAN JUAN BAUTISTA

San Juan Bautista State Historic Park: contains several historic structures, including the restored 1840 Castro House and the 1858 Plaza Hotel

SAN FRANCISCO

Hallidie Building: built by Willis Polk, 1918; credited as having the first glass-curtain wall, an 80-story sheer wall of glass with gothic trimmings

Ferry Building: 1898 gateway to the city, with a 235-foot tower

Old Mint: 1874 Greek Revival building and the oldest in the downtown area

City Hall: immense domed 1915 building containing the opera, ballet, symphony, and modern-art museums

Haas-Lilienthal House: built in 1886; striking Victorian architecture

Swedenborgian Church of the New Jerusalem: an 1895 building combining Italian and California architecture

Octagon House: example of interesting architectural theory

Vedanta Old Temple: early twentieth-century temple designed in a variety of international styles

Palace of Fine Arts: last remnant of the 1915 Panama-Pacific International Exhibition

The Presidio: the oldest continuously occupied army base in the western United States

Fort Point National Historic Site: mid-19th-century fortification below the Golden Gate Bridge

California Palace of the Legion of Honor: museum of French fine and decorative arts

San Francisco Museum of Modern Art: designed by Mario Botta in 1995; a Postmodern art museum with textured and patterned brickwork

Alamo Square: *see* pages 80–3

Golden Gate Bridge: *see* pages 129–36

Transamerica Pyramid: *see* page 170

ALCATRAZ ISLAND

Alcatraz: *see* pages 52–5

BENICIA

First State Capitol: used in 1852 for just thirteen months, the only surviving pre-Sacramento capitol

WOODSIDE

Filoli: 1916 eclectic-style house, designed by Willis Polk for a prominent San Franciscan

SAN JOSE AREA

Winchester Mystery House: built and continuously adapted from 1884 until 1922 due to a superstition that if building ceased, the owner would die

Rosicrucian Museum: designed in the rare Ancient-Egyptian style

SONOMA

Sonoma State Historic Park: historic Sonoma Plaza and restored historic homes including ***Lachryma Montis***—1850s home of General Vallejo—and the ***Buena Vista Winery,*** the oldest premium winery in the state

PETALUMA

Petaluma Adobe: one of the oldest preserved buildings in northern California

SACRAMENTO

Old Sacramento: historic sites including the restored 1855 courtroom

California State Capitol: restored Renaissance Revival capitol building and state offices, completed in 1894 at a cost of $2.4 million

SHASTA STATE HISTORIC PARK

Shasta: ruined town that was once the county seat and most prominent settlement

HORNITOS

Ghost town founded by Mexicans, which, during its heyday, held c.15,000 residents; contains an old jailhouse, Wells Fargo office, and general store

BODIE

Ghost Town: *see* page 51

FORT ROSS

A striking and dramatic reconstructed 1812 Russian settlement with a loghouse and Orthodox chapel

LOS ANGELES

El Pueblo de Los Angeles Historic Monument: preserved center of the old Spanish Settlement; includes the ***Avila Adobe,*** a reconstructed 1818 adobe replicating a Mexican cattleman's home of the 1840s; and the ***Plaza Substation,*** a 1904 power station for the streetcar system

First Interstate World Center (Library Tower): built 1990; the tallest building ever constructed in a major earthquake zone

777 Tower: designed by Cesar Pelli, an elegant 53-story-high structure of sculptured metal and glass

Watts Towers: designed by Simon Rodia, and built 1921–55

Bradbury Building: *see* pages 84–5

LA Public Library: *see* pages 110–11

Pacific Design Center: *see* page 172

HOLLYWOOD

Egyptian Theater: opened in 1922 as a re-creation of the Temple of Thebes

SANTA CATALINA ISLAND

Catalina Island Museum: housed in the Wrigley's 1929 Casino Building

PASADENA

Gamble House: *see* pages 96–7

SAN DIEGO

Balboa Park: center for the city's museums

Hotel Del Coronado: *see* pages 76–7

SAN LUIS REY

Mission San Luis Rey de Francia: the largest of the California missions; restored church

DEATH VALLEY NATIONAL PARK

Scotty's Castle: *see* pages 114–17

EUREKA

Carson Mansion: *see* pages 74–5

GARDEN GROVE

Crystal Cathedral: *see* pages 174–5

BERKELEY

First Church of Christ Scientist: designed by Bernard Maybeck (1910) with oriental, classical, Romanesque and Gothic motifs

PALO ALTO

Hanna Residence: a Frank Lloyd Wright house of 1936, designed entirely on a hexagon pattern

LA JOLLA

Salk Institute: designed by Louis I. Kahn from 1959–66

SAN RAFAEL

Marin County Civic Center: *see* pages 148–9

YOSEMITE NATIONAL PARK

Ahwahnee Hotel: *see* page 106

COLORADO

DENVER

Red Rocks Amphitheater: 9000-seater venue set between two 400-foot red-sandstone rocks

Denver Mint: 1904 Italian Renaissance style building modeled after a Florentine palace

Brown Palace Hotel: grand hotel opened in 1892 with a stunning atrium and elegant dining rooms

Denver Art Museum: stunning, fortress-like building designed by Gio Ponti

ASPEN

Wheeler Opera House: built in 1889 for magnate Jerome B. Wheeler; beautifully restored, vibrant interiors

LEADVILLE

Tabor Opera House: built in 1879, a brightly colored three-story opera house

COLORADO SPRINGS

Colorado Springs Pioneer Museum: located in the former El Paso County Courthouse (1903)

Air Force Academy Chapel: see page 157

CRIPPLE CREEK

Imperial Hotel: grand old hotel built in 1896

MESA VERDE NATIONAL PARK

Extensive Anasazi ruins of spectacular cliff dwellings constructed in alcoves high above the canyons

UTE MOUNTAIN TRIBAL PARK

Hundreds of spectacular cliff dwellings including the 80-room Lion House and the precarious Eagle's Nest

SILVERTON

An atmospheric mountain town with false-fronted stores, a courthouse, grand hotels, and magnificent Victorian homes

TELLURIDE

Former mining village; includes the San Miguel County Courthouse, 1887; New Sheridan Hotel & Opera House, a famous Telluride landmark, 1895; the Town Hall, 1883; and the Rio Grande Southern Railway Depot, 1891

CONNECTICUT

HARTFORD

State Capitol: opened in 1879; marble and granite, with a gold-leaf dome

Nook Farm: hilltop community with restored 1880s homes of Harriet Beecher Stowe and the ***Mark Twain House*** (*see* pages 66–7)

Old State House: designed by Charles Bulfinch, built in 1796, and the nation's oldest statehouse

NEW HAVEN

Yale University: founded in 1701 moved here in 1716; architecture includes the old buildings of the 1753 Connecticut Hall, and the 1842 Dwight Hall

Eli Whitney Museum: housed in an 1816 barn and restored gun factory

Peabody Museum of Natural History: new building dedicated in 1925

Yale University Art Gallery: main building (1953) designed by Louis I. Kahn

Christ Church on Broadway: built in 1897 in the English Gothic style with a red brick interior

Knights of Columbus Building: Roche-Dinkeloo, 1965–9

Ingalls Hockey Rink: *see* pages 150–1

MYSTIC

Mystic Seaport: reconstructed 17-acre waterfront village

NEW CANAAN

The Glass House: *see* page 144

DELAWARE

LEWES

Zwaanendael Museum: built in 1931 as a careful adaptation of the town hall in Hoorn, Holland

Lewes Historical Complex: several eighteenth-century hand-hewn homes

DOVER

Old State House: built 1792, its legislative chambers are now restored

Legislative Hall: the current state capitol, built 1932

Christ Episcopal Church: built in 1734

Kent County Courthouse: pretty 1874 structure, built on the site of the courthouse of 1691

NEW CASTLE

Immanuel Episcopal Church: built in 1703 and bordered by rows of two-hundred-year-old gravestones

Old Court House: built in 1732, served as the first state capitol

George Read II House: reconstruction of a large colonial house built 1797–1804

WILMINGTON

Old Town Hall: built in 1798; Federal-style structure restored to its classical beauty

Fort Christina: first permanent settlement in the Delaware Valley

Hendrickson House Museum: built in 1690 by Swedish farmer

Old Swedes Church: originally built in 1698–9; contains oldest known pulpit in the nation

BRANDYWINE VALLEY

Hagley Museum: the manor homes of the aristocratic Family, the du Ponts; includes the 1802 water-powered gunpowder mill along the banks of the Brandywine River; the Blacksmith Hill workers' community, the powder yards, a nineteenth-century machine shop, the du Pont's Georgian-style ***Eleutherian Mills*** residence, and the enormous pink ***Nemours Mansion***, 1910, modeled on the family's ancestral home in France

Winterthur: old du Pont family estate, now museum of early American decorative arts; each of its 200 rooms showcases a particular decorative style, from Shakers to North Carolina plantations

DISTRICT OF COLUMBIA

WASHINGTON, DC

Library of Congress: its magnificent Thomas Jefferson Building was opened in 1897, with a domed octagonal Reading Room, a 23-carat gold-plated dome, and elaborately decorated façade and interior

Supreme Court: current building (1935) designed by Cass Gilbert; acclaimed as a Corinthian masterpiece

Lincoln Memorial: dedicated in 1922, it is modeled upon a Doric temple

Washington Monument: a 555-foot marble obelisk; the tallest all-masonry structure in the world, completed in 1884

US Capitol: *see* pages 24–5

The Castle: the Smithsonian Institution's original home, a 1849 Norman-style building

Hirshhorn Museum: a 1974, Gordon Bunshaft/SOM-designed structure; a three-story cylinder supported on four massive concrete piers above a concrete plaza

National Museum of African Art: a curved and domed structure

National Museum of American Art: housed in the Greek Revival-style Old Patent Office

National Museum of American History: opened 1964; one of the last structures designed by McKim, Mead, and White

Corcoran Gallery of Art: includes the stunning *Salon Doré* (Gilded Room), which recreates an 18th-century Parisian interior with hand-carved paneling, gold-leaf decoration and ceiling murals

FBI: headquarters of the Federal Bureau of Investigation, housed in a fortress-like modern building

Ford's Theatre: beautiful reconstruction of a 19th-century playhouse
National Gallery of Art: includes IM Pei's modernistic East Building of 1978, and the original Neoclassical gallery, designed by John Russell Pope in 1941
United States Holocaust Memorial Museum: *see* page 180
The White House: Neoclassical structure, completed in 1800 by Irish immigrant James Hoban, who modeled it on the Georgian manors of Dublin
Union Station: *see* page 98
Jefferson Memorial: completed in 1943 and modeled on his country home, Monticello, a dome supported by an Ionic colonnade

FLORIDA

Orlando

Walt Disney World®: massive entertainment complex including the **EPCOT Discovery Center**, *see* page 163

St. Petersburg and Bradenton

Sunshine Skyway Bridge: completed in 1987, a 29,040-foot-long bridge, painted bright yellow

Boca Raton

Cloister Inn: designed by Addison Mizner; opened in 1926 at a cost of $1.25 million, the most expensive 100-room hotel ever built at the time; designed in a pseudo-Spanish style with courtyards

Palm Beach

Whitehall: also known as the *Flagler Museum*, fronted by white Doric columns it is an overtly ostentatious home
The Breakers Hotel: built in 1926 in the style of an Italianate palace

St. Augustine

Castillo de San Marcos: fortress started in the late 1600s
Lightner Museum: the former *Alcazar Hotel,* an 1889 Spanish Renaissance Revival style structure
The Oldest House: the Gonzales-Alvarez house; dates from the early 1700s

Miami

Villa Vizcaya: built in 1914 at a cost of $15 million; re-creates a 16th-century Italian villa
Biltmore Hotel: fabulous 1926 building with a 26-story tower
Freedom Tower: built in 1925 and modeled on a Spanish bell tower

Key Biscane

Cape Florida lighthouse: 95-foot structure built in the 1820s
Bass Museum of Fine Art: Art Deco building by Russell Pancoast (1930)
South Beach Deco district: pastel-colored '20s and '30s buildings; includes *The Greystone,* a Henry Hohauser's masterpiece; *The Essex House*, a hotel completed in 1938; and the *Century Hotel* (*see* page 121); includes the famous *Ocean Drive*, ten blocks of pastel-colored buildings such as the renowned Cardozo, Carlyle, Cavalier, and Breakwater Hotels

Pensacola

North Hill: contains elaborate homes of 1870–1930, in a plethora of styles

Sarasota

Ringling Museum Complex: the Venetian Gothic mansion, *Ca' d'Zan*

Pass-a-Grille

Don Cesar Hotel: luxurious grandiose pink castle, opened in 1928

Tampa

Plant Hall, University of Tampa: formerly the Tampa Bay Hotel, built at a cost of $3 million (1890)

GEORGIA

Atlanta

High Museum of Art: white glass-and-steel building opened in 1983
Underground Atlanta: a subterranean maze of cobbled gas-lit streets; the original site of the city
Michael C. Carlos Museum, Emory University: stylish museum designed by Michael Graves
One Atlantic Center: tall, spiky, futuristic building
Herndon Home: 1910 Beaux Arts house, designed and lived in by freed slave Alonzo Herndon
Georgia Dome: completed in 1992 at a cost of $214 million
One Peachtree Center: designed by John Portman & Assoc, it is 867 feet high
Westin Peachtree Plaza Hotel: 723-foot tower designed by John Portman; originally held a lake in the lobby
Atlanta History Center: the Swan House, a 1920s mock-classical mansion
Fox Theater: *see* page 120
Hyatt Regency Hotel: *see* page 165

Brunswick

Hofwyl-Broadfield Plantation: nineteenth-century antebellum plantation

Jekyll Island

Originally bought in 1887 for use by a select few, including the Rockefellers, Pulitzers, Macys, and Vanderbilts, whose opulent houses remain

St. Simon's Island

Fort Frederica National Monument: built in 1736 as the largest British fort in North America

Ocmulgee National Monument

Site of Mississippian culture settlement AD 900–1100

Savannah

Historic District: examples of architecture of the 18th and 19th centuries
Hermitage Plantation: *see* page 44

Fort Pulaski National Monument

A Confederate stronghold, set on its own island and ringed by a moat

HAWAII

Honolulu

Iolani Palace: the official residence of Hawaii's last king (1882)
Kawaihao Church: dedicated in 1842, made from thousands of coral blocks
Honolulu Academy of Arts: designed in 1927 to combine the appearance of a traditional Hawaiian structure with the plan of a modern museum
Queen Emma Summer Palace: elegant home built in 1847

Hanalei

Waioli Mission House: built by New England missionaries in 1836; restored with period furnishings and artifacts

Lahaina

Pioneer Hotel: One of Hawaii's two oldest hotels, built 1901
Lahaina Courthouse: built 1859 of stones originally used for King Kamehameha III's palace

Hilo

Lyman Museum: the original 1830s Mission House, furnished in *koa* wood

Kawaihae

Puukohola Heiau National Historic Site: temple built by Kamehameha I (1791)

Puuhonua o Honaunau National Historical Park

Grounds include a palace and three *heiaus,* guarded by large carved effigies of gods; also includes *Ka Lae*, with temple remnants dating to AD 700

Hawaii Volcanoes National Park

Star of the Sea Church: interior of vividly colored murals painted in the 1920s

Hawi

Old-style plantation town virtually unchanged since its hey-day

IDAHO

Coeur d'Alene

Coeur d'Alene Resort: hotel which boasts the world's only floating golf green
Mission of the Sacred Heart: Idaho's oldest public building, built 1850–3

Nez Percé National Historical Park

Contains 24 sites displaying Nez Percé heritage

Idaho City

Quaint small town with classic western storefronts

POCATELLO

Fort Hall: a trading post on the Oregon Trail, with period features

CHESTERFIELD

An early Mormon settlement along the Oregon Trail founded in 1881

BOISE

Fort Boise: for the protection of pioneers on the Oregon Trail (1862)

ARCO

Experimental Breeder Reactor No 1: the world's first nuclear power station

IDAHO FALLS

Features the prominent landmark of the 1945 Idaho Falls Mormon Temple

ILLINOIS

CHICAGO

Wacker Drive: many diverse structures such as the Beaux Arts *Jewelers Building*, 1926, and *333 W. Wacker Drive* (*see* pages 176–7)

IBM Building: Ludwig Mies van der Rohe's huge 1971 masterpiece

Merchandise Mart: the world's largest building on its opening in 1931

Chicago Board of Trade: contained in a stunning Art Deco tower

The Rookery: built in 1886 with a Moorish Gothic exterior, and a lobby of Italian marble and gold leaf

Reliance Building: see page 87

Carson Pirie Scott store: a grand turn-of-the-century department store (1889)

Sears Tower: see page 171

Old Town: St. Michael's Church (1873); century-old rowhouses and cottages

Field Museum of Natural History, a huge Burnham-designed Greek temple-style building

Michigan Avenue: includes landmarks such as the 1920 *Drake Hotel*, the *Wrigley Building* (*see* pages 118–9); the *Tribune Tower*, completed in 1925; and the 1970 *John Hancock Tower* (*see* pages 167–69)

Historic Water Tower: stone castle, topped by a 100-foot tower, built in 1869

Glessner House: Chicago's only surviving H.H. Richardson-designed house, built in 1886

University of Chicago: includes the huge, Gothic Rockefeller Memorial Chapel, and Frank Lloyd Wright's *Robie House* (*see* pages 100-01)

O'Hare International Airport: see pages 152–53

Marina City: see page 164

WEST SIDE AND OAK PARK

Oak Park: c.1900 suburb, preserved as a national historic district; a number of buildings designed by Frank Lloyd Wright, including *Unity Temple* (1906) and the *Frank Lloyd Wright Home and Studio* (1889)

SPRINGFIELD

Old State Capitol: center of state government 1839–76

Illinois State Capitol: grand structure, built 1868–88

Dana-Thomas House: example of Frank Lloyd Wright's Prairie houses (1904)

COLLINSVILLE

Cahokia Mounds State Historic Site: includes 109 Prehistoric mounds

WILMETTE

Bahá'í House of Worship: nine-sided domed building completed in 1953

PLANO

Farnsworth House: see page 145

INDIANA

COLUMBUS

Church in Columbus: designed by Eliel Saarinen in 1940

NEW HARMONY

The Atheneum: designed by Richard Meier, 1975–9; stunning structure with porcelain enameled cladding

MICHIGAN CITY

Barker Mansion: an opulent 38-room Victorian home, built by a founding father of the rail car industry

CROWN POINT

"Grand Old Lady": beautiful Lake County Courthouse, built 1878

NAPPANEE

Amish Acres Historic Farmstead: Amish farm lands and buildings from 1839

FOUNTAIN CITY

Levi Coffin State Historic Site: Federal style brick home built in 1839

INDIANAPOLIS

Monument Circle: a series of memorials and plazas dedicated to veterans

Lockerbie Square Historic District: cobblestone streets of multicolored wood-frame cottages

Indianapolis Speedway: home to the legendary Indianapolis 500

College Life Insurance Co.: designed by Roche-Dinkeloo from 1967–71

BLOOMINGTON

Indiana University Art Museum: designed by I. M. Pei & partners

MADISON

Lanier Mansion State Historic Site: 1844 Greek Revival house and gardens

LINCOLN CITY

Lincoln Boyhood National Memorial: re-creation of a pioneer homestead

EVANSVILLE

Reitz Home Museum: a restored French Second Empire mansion

IOWA

COUNCIL BLUFFS

Historic General Dodge House: the 1869 home of railroader and Civil War General Grenville M. Dodge

Historic Pottowattamie County Jail: built in 1888 and used as jail until 1969

DES MOINES

Iowa State Capitol: completed 1886, topped with a gold leaf dome, boasts marbled corridors and Venetian glass mosaics

MCGREGOR

Effigy Mounds National Monument: contains 195 prehistoric mounds

DUBUQUE

Mathias Ham House Historic Site: stately mansion of one of the town's earliest settlers

AMANA COLONIES

Communal religious villages founded in 1855 by pacifist German refugees

IOWA CITY

Old Capitol: grand, gold-domed building that served as state capitol 1842–57

WEST BRANCH

Herbert Hoover National Historic Site: a recreated 1870s Quaker farming village, including the 1874 cottage where Hoover was born; his father's blacksmith shop; a schoolhouse; a Quaker Meetinghouse; and the Presidential Library-Museum which presents his life and public career

MUSCATINE

Muscatine Art Center: housed in a grand 1908 mansion

MOUNT PLEASANT

Harlan-Lincoln House: built 1870s by U. S. Senator James Harlan

FORT MADISON

Old Fort Madison: recreated fort, built in 1808 as exchange post

SIOUX CITY

Woodbury County Courthouse: see pages 108–9

KANSAS

NICODEMUS

Nicodemus National Historic Site: African-American post-Civil War town

DODGE CITY

Historic Fort Dodge: 1860s buildings, with a museum

HAYS

Fort Hays State Historic Site: built 1867 and abandoned 1889; includes a blockhouse, officer's quarters, and guardhouse

LARNED

Fort Larned National Historic Site: restored military base established in 1859

ABILENE

Old Abilene Town: a replica of the town during its cattle boom

COUNCIL GROVE

Kaw Mission State Historic Site and Museum: an 1851 boarding school

TOPEKA

Brown v. Board of Education National Historic Site: includes the Monroe Elementary School

Historic Ward-Meade Park: an 1870s mansion, botanical gardens, and reconstructed turn-of-the-century town square

FORT SCOTT

Fort Scott National Historic Site: 20 French Colonial structures with exteriors restored to 1840s appearance and several historically furnished rooms

KENTUCKY

PLEASANT HILL

Shaker Village: established by Shaker missionaries from New England in 1805

CORBIN

Kentucky Fried Chicken: the original restaurant of "Colonel" Harlan Sanders; restored with 1940s decor and memorabilia

STEARNS

A classic former mining company town, in which the company owned every building, from stores and the church to the sheriff's office

LEXINGTON

Transylvania University: redbrick, ivy-covered buildings of 1780

HODGENVILLE

Abraham Lincoln's birthplace: one-room cabin, now National Historic Site

LORETTO

Maker's Mark Distillery: a collection of beautifully restored black, red and gray plankhouses, in which whiskey is still made manually

FORT KNOX

Bullion Depository: bomb-proof structure, surrounded by security fences, machine-gun turrets, patrol guards and huge floodlights; stores nine million pounds of the federal gold reserve behind doors weighing 20 tons

LOUISVILLE

Humana Building: *see* page 178

LOUISIANA

BATON ROUGE

Louisiana State Capitol: Art Deco building in 50 acres of showpiece gardens

Old State Capitol: in use from 1850–1932; referred to by Mark Twain as "that monstrosity on the Mississippi," it resembles both a castle and a cathedral

LSU Rural Life Museum: re-creates pre-industrial Louisiana life with restored buildings including a plantation house, slave cottages, and sugar mill

Nottoway: the largest surviving plantation home in the South

SUNSET

Chretien Point Plantation: built 1831; Louisiana's oldest Greek Revival building; featured in *Gone with the Wind*

EDGARD

San Francisco House: built in the Steamboat Gothic style, its elaborate façade was designed to re-create the ambience of a Mississippi showboat

VACHERIE

Laura Plantation: stunning Creole sugar-cane plantation mansion, built 1805, painted red and yellow

Oak Alley: *see* page 45

NEW ORLEANS

Old Ursuline Convent: only intact French colonial structure in the city (1745)

Gallier House: designed by architect James Gallier, Jr. (1857)

Esplanade Avenue: a boulevard lined with 19th-century Creole mansions

St. Louis Cathedral: the oldest continuously active cathedral in the United States (1794); dominated by three tall slate steeples

Cabildo: built as the Casa Capitular, seat of the Spanish colonial government; impressive colonnade, fan windows and wrought-iron balconies

Presbytère: designed as a rectory; completed in 1813; served as a courthouse

Pontalba Buildings: 19th-century three-story colonnaded structures, commissioned by Baroness Pontalba; innovative in their use of cast iron

Custom House: headquarters to Union General Butler, and prison for Confederate soldiers of the Civil War; the classical exterior gives way to a huge marble hall, illuminated by a 55-foot skylight, with 14 columns of Italian marble supporting the white and gilt ceiling

Superdome: home of the New Orleans Saints football team; covering 52 acres, with 27 stories and a diameter of 680 feet

Confederate Museum: Romanesque Revival building of 1891, originally constructed as a place for Confederate veterans to display their mementos

St. Charles Avenue: 1941 replica of Tara, the house in *Gone with the Wind*, and the Wedding Cake House, a Colonial-Greek Revival building

New Orleans Museum of Art: opened in 1911, Classically inspired building

Shotgun Houses: constructed 1850–1910, the predominant New Orleans structures of their time have wooden exteriors and front porches supported by pillars and brackets ornamented with Victorian lacy motifs

CANE IVER ROADS

Melrose: plantation home, granted in 1794 to Marie Coincoin, a freed slave

NATCHITOCHES

The oldest European settlement in Louisiana, begun as a French trading post in 1714; restored Creole architecture; the 1717 ***Immaculate Conception Catholic Church***, and ***Fort St. Jean Baptist*** (1716, reconstruction)

MAINE

PASSAMAQUODDY BAY

Saint Croix Island International Historic site: one of the earliest European settlements on the North Atlantic coast of North America (est. 1604)

WEST QUODDY HEAD

The easternmost point of the United States; 1808 striped lighthouse with visitor center; 1830 settlement of Bailey's Mistake, named for a sea captain who beached his lumber vessel here

MACHIAS

Burnham Tavern: where the first naval attack of the Revolutionary War was planned in 1775; the oldest standing building in eastern Maine (1770)

BELFAST

Waterfront historic district: whitewashed Greek Revival houses

WISCASSET

Castle Tucker Museum: Federal-style mansion built in 1807

BRUNSWICK

Harriet Beecher Stowe House

Joshua L. Chamberlain Museum

Skolfield-Whittier House: 17-roomed home, built 1925

PORTLAND

Wadsworth-Longfellow House: first brick house in Portland, built by Henry Longfellow's grandfather in 1785–86; the poet's childhood home

Portland Museum of Art: housed designed by I.M. Pei & Partners (1983)

Victoria Mansion/Morse-Libby House: built 1858–60, Italian villa-style house

Portland Observatory: 86-foot-high signal tower (1807)

CAPE ELIZABETH

Portland Head Light: *see* pages 26–7

MARYLAND

ANNAPOLIS

Maryland State House: completed in 1779, served as an early capitol of the United States; grounds encompass the Old Treasury Building built (1735)

Hammond-Harwood House: redbrick Palladian villa (1774) designed by William Buckland
William Paca House: built 1765
Shiplap House: 1715, originally a tavern, now a small museum
Market House: an early 19th-century replacement of a colonial warehouse used by the Revolutionary army

ST. MARY'S CITY

Reconstruction of Maryland's first colonial capital, established here in 1634

BALTIMORE

City Hall: 1867, French Second Empire style building
Oriole Park at Camden Yards: stadium of the Baltimore Orioles, opened in 1992 on site of former railroad center, two blocks from the birthplace of the legendary George Herman "Babe" Ruth; designed by Kansas City architects Helmuth, Obata and Kassabaum
PSI Net Stadium: massive 69,300-seat structure, designed by Helmuth, Obata and Kassabaum; opened in 1998 as home to the Baltimore Ravens
Flag House and 1812 Museum: where, in 1813, Mary Pickersgill sewed the 30- by 45-foot U.S. flag that inspired Francis Scott Key to write *The Star-Spangled Banner*
Peabody Library: famed for its interior; a skylit atrium rises above five tiers of intricate wrought-iron balconies
Walters Art Gallery: palazzo-like building, opened to public in 1909
B&O Railroad Museum: housed in an 1830 passenger depot
Senator Theatre: opened c. 1939; Art Deco movie house, still in operation
Phoenix Shot Tower: *see* page 41

HAVRE DE GRACE

Concord Point Light: oldest continuously operating lighthouse in the US (1827)

ST. MICHAELS

Hooper Strait Lighthouse: screwpile cottage-style lighthouse, originally built in 1879 on Tangier Sound; deactivated and moved here in 1966

CUMBERLAND

Canal Place: western terminus of the C&O (Chesapeake and Ohio) Canal, an impressive engineering feat begun in 1813 but not completed until 1850, by which time the railroads had made it obsolete
Washington Street Historic District: the Allegany County Courthouse; Allegany County Library; and Emmanuel Episcopal Church
George Washington's Headquarters: one room cabin used by George Washington as a young aide to General Braddock; built 1754-55
National Road & Toll House: constructed in 1811, the National Road was the first federally funded road

THURMONT

Camp David: established in 1942 as a retreat for Franklin D. Roosevelt, located in Catoctin Mountain Park

MASSACHUSETTS

DEDHAM

Fairbanks House: the first section was built c.1636; the oldest surviving timber frame house in North America

LINCOLN

Gropius House: built in 1938 by and for Walter Gropius, director of Germany's Bauhaus School

HANCOCK SHAKER VILLAGE

An outdoor history museum concerning the life of the Shakers, 1783 to 1960; includes the ***Round Barn*** (*see* pages 36–9)

STOCKBRIDGE

Naumkeag: 26-room gabled mansion, designed by Stanford White in 1885

OLD STURBRIDGE VILLAGE

Museum, re-creating a rural New England town of the 1830s

WORCESTER

Higgins Armory Museum: *see* pages 122–3

LOWELL

Lowell National Historical Park: includes *Lowell Textile Mills* (*see* pages 46–7)

MINUTE MAN NATIONAL HISTORICAL PARK

Preserves ***The Wayside Home of Authors***, more than 300 years old, home of Nathaniel Hawthorne, Louisa May Alcott and Margaret Sidney

SALEM

Salem Maritime National Historic Site: 12 historic waterfront structures
House of the Seven Gables: inspiration for Nathaniel Hawthorne's famed novel; a 1688 three-story mansion
Derby House: Georgian Colonial house built c.1762 for Elias Hasket Derby, America's first millionaire

SAUGUS

Saugus Iron Works National Historic Site: site of the first integrated iron-works in North America, 1646–68; includes working waterwheels

CAMBRIDGE

Harvard Houses: upperclassmen's residences; includes underground tunnels decorated with the graffiti of past residents in ***St. Adams House***, the blue-topped bell tower of ***Lowell House***, the purple spire of ***Eliot House***, and ***Dunster House***, with its famed red Georgian tower top, modeled on Christchurch College in Oxford
Harvard Yard: created in 1636 as a grazing field for university livestock; includes Hollis Hall (1762); Matthews Hall (c.1862); Memorial Church; Harvard's Science Center; Harvard Law School's ***Austin Hall*** (*see* page 69); and the Le Corbusier Carpenter Center
Massachusetts Institute of Technology: features interesting architecture including Eero Saarinen's Kresge Auditorium and the MIT Chapel; and I. M. Pei's Weisner Building
Hooper-Lee-Nichols House: 1685 farmhouse, remodeled 1742

BOSTON

Boston City Hall: designed by Kallman, McKinnell and Knowles, 1963–68
Boston Public Library: originally designed by McKim Mead & White and built in 1895 in the Renaissance Revival style; includes a marble grand staircase, decorated ceilings, and an open-air central courtyard modeled after the Palazzo della Chancelleria in Rome
Carpenter Center for the Visual Arts: built 1964, the only building in the U.S. designed solely by Le Corbusier, and also the last of his career
Christian Science buildings: world headquarters of the First Church of Christ, Scientist, designed by I.M. Pei, 1974
Commonwealth Avenue: tree-lined street modeled after the boulevards of Paris; contains the 1904 ***Baylies Mansion***; the 1872 ***Ames-Webster Mansion***; the 1899 ***Burrage House***; and the 1872 ***First Baptist Church of Boston***, designed by H.H. Richardson
New Old South Church: Italian Gothic structure (1875)
Arlington Street Church: Italianesque masterpiece (1861) with a wealth of Tiffany stained-glass windows
Bay Village: one of the oldest sections of Boston
Boston Athenæum: established 1807, moved here in 1849; designed by Edward Clarke Cabota as a replica of the Palazzo da Porta Festa in Vicenza, Italy
Custom House Tower: built in 1847 and surrounded by 32 huge Doric columns, with a thirty-story Greek Revival tower added in 1915
Grain and Flour Exchange Building: Coolidge's 1893 fortresslike building, with a turreted conical roof, encircled by a series of pointed dormers; and several Bulfinch Federal-style mercantile buildings
Omni Parker House: hotel that has hosted world luminaries since 1856; Ho Chi Minh and Malcolm X each used to wait tables in the restaurant
Boston Old City Hall: a French Second Empire building built 1865; served as Boston's City Hall until 1969
Old Corner Bookstore: built in 1712, and one of Boston's oldest structures
Boston University: includes ***Myles Standish Hall***, a scaled-down version of New York's Flatiron Building

North Square: includes the ***Paul Revere House***, the oldest residential address in the city (c. 1680); the oldest brick house in Boston (1710); and the 1723 ***Old North Church***, the oldest church in Boston
Massachusetts State House: *see* page 32
Old State House: *see* page 33
Faneuil Hall: *see* pages 34–5
Trinity Church: *see* page 68
John Hancock Tower: *see* page166
PLYMOUTH
Plimoth Plantation: Pilgrim village of 1627 and Wampanoag settlement

MICHIGAN

ANN ARBOR
Power Center: 1,450-seat theater designed by Roche-Dinkeloo, 1965–71;
MACKINAC ISLAND
Site of a French mission to the Huron, 1670–71; a French fort in 1715; a base for the American Fur Company; a jail for Confederate officers during the Civil War; the restored ***Fort Mackinac*** was a U.S. Army outpost until 1890
HOLLAND
Settled 1847 by Dutch religious dissidents; includes clog factory and windmill
DETROIT
Detroit Institute of Arts: the 19th-century structure houses the sixth-largest museum in the United States
Museum of African-American History: founded in 1965, the world's largest African-American museum
Renaissance Center: six gleaming towers with an observation deck
Fox Theatre: a restored Siamese-Byzantine movie palace, opened in 1928
Henry Ford Museum: Museum of Americana with transportation exhibits
Greenfield Village: relocated houses of famous Americans; includes Henry Ford's birthplace, the Wright Brothers' cycle shop, and Edison's laboratory;
Pewabic Pottery: *see* page 92
BLOOMFIELD HILLS
Cranbrook Academy of Art: *see* page 128

MINNESOTA

OWATONNA
National Farmers' Bank: designed by Louis H. Sullivan, 1907–08, to resemble a giant treasure chest for the safekeeping of depositors' money
COLLEGEVILLE
St. John's Abbey: designed by Marcel Breuer, 1953–61
DULUTH
St. Louis County Heritage and Arts Center: constructed in 1892 in the French-Norman style; served as the depot for seven rail lines in 1910
GRAND PORTAGE
Grand Portage National Monument: includes a stockade, a great hall, a kitchen, warehouse, fur trade museum, and an Ojibwa cultural center
MINNEAPOLIS-ST. PAUL
Alexander Ramsey House: well-preserved Victorian-era home
Historic Fort Snelling: 1820s military outpost
James J. Hill House: majestic red sandstone home of the builder of the Great Northern Railway; tours demonstrate servant life in the Gilded Age
Minnesota History Center: an architectural masterpiece that offers views of downtown and the State Capitol
American Swedish Institute: museum and cultural center housed in a turn-of-the-century mansion
Sibley House Historic Site: one of the state's oldest settlements, limestone buildings dated 1820s–50s
IDS Center: landmark tower, built in 1973, designed by Philip Johnson
Norwest Center: *see* page 173
Frederick R. Weisman Art Museum: *see* page 179

MISSISSIPPI

BILOXI
Old Biloxi: historic buildings include the 1895 Brielmaier House, the 1835 Old French House, The 1896 Romanesque Revival old People's Bank, and the 1908 Neoclassical City Hall
Magnolia Hotel: one of the oldest Gulf Coast hotels dating to the 1840s
DuBuys House: c.1840 Creole cottage
Beauvoir: white cottage, final home of Confederate President Jefferson Davis
WEST SHIP ISLAND
Fort Massachusetts: giant D-shaped fortification, built 1859
OXFORD
Rowan Oak: former home of William Faulkner; built in 1840
Neilson's: an old-fashioned department store
TUPELO
Elvis Presley Birthplace: a two-room shotgun house, built for $150 in 1934
JACKSON
Old Capitol: structure with a portico and rotunda, completed in 1840
Mississippi State Capitol: far more ornate than its predecessor, built in 1903, Beaux Arts style; notably, the gilt eagle atop the dome looks away from Washington
Governor's Mansion: built 1842, with portico of Corinthian columns
Lamar Life Building: erected 1924–25, Jackson's first skyscraper
NATCHEZ
Stanton Hall: 1858 palatial mansion fronted by tall Corinthian columns
Grand Village: ceremonial mounds and dwellings of the local Natchez
Dunleith: plantation house, built 1856
Elmscourt: *see* page 48
Longwood: *see* page 49
VICKSBURG
Old Court House Museum: Greek Revival edifice built in 1858
Balfour House: built 1835 in the Greek Revival style
Martha Vick House: handsome Greek Revival house,1830s

MISSOURI

KANSAS CITY
Kemper Arena: designed by Helmut Jahn in 1974
Kelly's Westport Inn: built 1837, the city's oldest structure
INDEPENDENCE
Harry S. Truman National Historic Site: his home from 1919 until his death
ST. LOUIS
Jefferson National Expansion Memorial: Eero Saarinen's ***Gateway Arch*** (*see* pages 158–61); the Museum of Westward Expansion, a detailed look at the Lewis and Clark expedition; and the Old Courthouse, one of the oldest standing buildings in St. Louis, begun in 1839
Union Station: Romanesque structure with a 230-foot clock tower (1894)
Ulysses S Grant National Historic Site: includes the 1855 main house
Anheuser-Busch plant: largest brewery in the world
Forest Park: contains the Beaux Arts St. Louis Art Museum, the only surviving structure from the 1904 World's Fair
Wainwright Building: *see* page 86
Priory Chapel: *see* page 156
ST. CHARLES
First Missouri State Capitol State Historic Site: Federal-style brick building
DEFIANCE
Daniel Boone Home: the frontiersman's Georgian mansion built 1805–10
JEFFERSON CITY
State Capitol: completed in 1917; famous for its murals by Thomas Hart Benton and its great dome
Jefferson Landing State Historic Site: 19th-century riverside buildings
Cole County Historical Society: 1871 row house

BRANSON

Inspiration Tower: opened in 1989, it is the tallest structure of its kind made entirely of prestressed concrete

MONTANA

GREAT FALLS

Cascade County Courthouse: a 1903 Tudor Revival structure with a copper dome

KALISPELL

Conrad Mansion: a three-story, Shingle-style house built in 1895

SAINT IGNATIUS

Saint Ignatius Mission: established in 1854, the present brick mission dates to 1891, built in a High Victorian Gothic style

MISSOULA

Missoula County Courthouse: 1910 sandstone building; Beaux Arts and Classical Revival styles

Fort Missoula: established 1877 to protect settlers to the area

DEER LODGE

Grant-Kohrs Ranch National Historic Site: preserved buildings of a pioneering ranch complex started in 1862

ANACONDA

Washoe Theater: Art Deco movie palace,1936

HELENA

State Capitol: Neoclassical structure with murals by Charles Russell

Cathedral of St. Helena: its majestic red-tiled spires rise 230 feet

LIVINGSTON

Depot Center: built 1902 by the Northern Pacific Railroad; designed by Reed & Stem of the Grand Central Terminal, New York

BANNACK

The first territorial capital of Montana, abandoned in 1938; now a ghost town

BILLINGS

Moss Mansion: designed in 1903 by Henry J. Hardenburgh, the architect of New York's Plaza Hotel and the original Waldorf-Astoria

WIBAUX

St. Peter's Catholic Church: dedicated in 1885, enlarged using native lava rock

FORT UNION TRADING POST NATIONAL HISTORIC SITE

Built in 1829 by the American Fur Company

NEBRASKA

FORT ROBINSON STATE PARK

Preserved 1874 fort site where the U.S. Army campaigned against the Sioux; includes site of the killing of Crazy Horse (1877)

SIDNEY

Fort Sidney: established in 1867

NORTH PLATTE

Buffalo Bill Ranch Historical Park: a property of William "Buffalo Bill" Cody

KEARNEY

Fort Kearney State Historic Park: established in 1847, the first military post along the Oregon Trail

RED CLOUD

Willa Cather State Historic Site: offers tours of buildings in Cather's novels

FORT CALHOUN

Fort Atkinson State Historical Park: site of the first formal meetings between Lewis & Clark and Native Americans (1804); first U.S. military post west of the Missouri River, 1820

LINCOLN

Nebraska state capitol: 1932 building by Bertram Goodhue with 400-foot central tower, topped by a 20-foot statue of a sower

BEATRICE

Homestead National Monument of America: a pioneer cabin and schoolhouse

NEVADA

AUSTIN

A ghost town featuring ***Stokes Castle***, an 1897 architectural oddity

RHYOLITE

Ghost town; includes the ***Las Vegas and Tonopah Railroad Depot***, and the ***Bottle House***, constructed of whisky bottles

EUREKA

Eureka Opera House: 1879, with brick-and-iron fireproof front and a shock-absorbing dance floor, advanced technology for its time

VIRGINIA CITY

Saint Mary's in the Mountains: rebuilt Gothic Revival church (1875)

BERLIN

Berlin Knickerbocker 30 Stamp Mill: restored tall wooden structure

LAS VEGAS

The legendary "strip" has four miles of casinos

HOOVER DAM: *see* page 137

PIOCHE

A ghost town and the most notorious mining camp in Nevada; features the **Million Dollar Courthouse**, built in 1871 at such expense that it was not paid off until 1937; now houses a museum of local history

NEW HAMPSHIRE

HANOVER

Hood Museum of Art: Postmodern building designed by Charles Moore and Chad Floyd, 1981–3

PORTSMOUTH

John Paul Jones House: 1758 gambrel-roofed clapboard house

Moffatt-Ladd House: 1763 three-story mansion

St. John's Church: 1809; George Washington attended services in the original structure in 1789

Warner House: the first brick mansion built in New England, 1716

Wentworth-Gardner House: built 1760

Gov. John Langdon House: 1784 colonial governor's mansion and gardens

Rundlet-May House: Federal-style home, built 1807

Portsmouth Athenaeum: Federal-style building with a library

Strawbery Banke: 10 preserved acres of the town's original site; includes the *Drisco House*, where each individual room dates from a different era; the 1766 *Pitt Tavern*; and the *Dinsmore Shop*, where a cooper manufactures barrels with the tools and methods of 1800

LACONIA

Belknap Mill: claims to be "the oldest unaltered brick textile mill building in the United States"

CONCORD

State Capitol: constructed 1816–18 of granite from local quarries

MANCHESTER

Zimmerman House: Frank Lloyd Wright-designed Usonian house (1950)

CANTERBURY SHAKER VILLAGE

Shaker community founded by Ann Lee in the 1780s, 300-strong by 1860; includes the 1792 meeting house

CORNISH

Saint-Gaudens National Historic Site: includes the 1885–1907 home, gardens and studios of sculptor Augustus Saint-Gaudens

NEW JERSEY

BAYONNE

Bayonne Bridge: one of the longest steel arch bridges in the world (1931)

MOUNT HOLLY

Old School House: oldest schoolhouse in the state (1756)

PATERSON

The Great Falls Cultural and Historic Center: Manufacturing complex

PRINCETON

Princeton University: the nation's fourth oldest; encompasses the Grad College, Whig Hall, Woodrow Wilson School, and chapel; the Gordon Wu Hall, by Robert Venturi (1983), is acclaimed for its 'considerate' design

MATAWAN

Burrows Mansion: built in 1723, an elegant Georgian mansion

MONTCLAIR

Evergreen House: built in 1896 blending Tudor and Colonial Revival styles

ATLANTIC CITY

Created as a rail terminal resort in 1854; boasts the nation's first Boardwalk (1870), and the world's first Big Wheel (1869); grand old hotels have been largely replaced by casinos

CAPE MAY

The whole old town is a National Historic Landmark, with more than 600 Victorian buildings

PARK RIDGE

Wortendyke Barn: one of the last examples of the New World Dutch barns

NEW MEXICO

SANTA FE

Palace of the Governors: continuously used since 1610

Santuario de Guadalupe: mission church from the late 18th century

PECOS

Pecos National Historic Park: 15th-century pueblo of Pecos; two missions

SANTA CLARA PUEBLO

Puye Cliff Dwellings: constructed between AD 600 and c.1580

CHIMAYO

Santuario de Chimayo: twin-towered adobe church built around 1814

CHACO CULTURE NATIONAL HISTORICAL PARK

Complex of more than 2,000 Anasazi ruins, from the tenth century

AZTEC

Aztec Ruins National Monument: large and well-preserved Anasazi ruins of a 500-room pueblo, c. 1110, with restored kiva

TAOS

La Hacienda de Don Antonio Severino Martinez: period adobe residence

TAOS PUEBLO: SEE PAGES 16–17

RANCHOS DE TAOS: SEE PAGE 19

FORT UNION NATIONAL MONUMENT

The largest fort in the American Southwest, established 1851

ACOMA PUEBLO

Also called Sky City, one of the oldest continuously inhabited villages in the United States

EL MORRO NATIONAL MONUMENT

Remains of the 1275 Atsinna Pueblo; also the 200-foot *Inscription Rock*

GILA CLIFF DWELLINGS NATIONAL MONUMENT

An ancient pueblo inhabited since about 1280

SALINAS PUEBLO MISSIONS NATIONAL MONUMENT

Quarai: 1628 mission, chapel and Native American pueblo

Abó: ruins of the beautiful Mission of San Gregorio de Abó

Gran Quivira: prehistoric pueblo with the Mission of San Buenaventura

NEW YORK

NEW YORK CITY

Waldorf Astoria: grand Art Deco landmark, 1929, moved from its original location, which was acquired for the Empire State Building, and reopened as "the world's grandest and largest hotel" in 1931

Brooklyn Children's Museum: underground structure built in 1977; uses building structures in its design, such as the trolley kiosk entrance hall

Chase Manhattan Bank: Gordon Bunshaft/SOM, 1961; one of the tallest structures in Lower Manhattan

Citicorp Center: built 1978, the first skyscraper in the U.S. to contain a pendulum-like device to stabilize the building against high winds

Daily News Building: c. 1930 tall building with an Art Deco entrance

Everson Museum of Art: designed by I. M. Pei (1968)

Guggenheim Museum: designed by Frank Lloyd Wright (1956–9)

McGraw-Hill Building: designed by Raymond Hood in 1930, often referred to as the "jolly green giant" due to its blue-green glass cladding

New York Racquet Club: designed as a Renaissance Revival building by McKim, Mead, and White (1916–9); based on an Italian palazzo

Rose Center for Earth and Space: shimmering, glass-encased transparent structure, opened in 2000

Seagram Building: Ludwig Mies van der Rohe, 1954–8; a 37-story bronze-and glass structure, considered America's first glass skyscraper.

George Washington Bridge: the world's only 14-lane suspension bridge, opened in 1927

Brooklyn Bridge: see pages 70–1

Statue of Liberty: see page 72–3

Plaza Hotel: see page 93

Flatiron Building: see page 94

New York Stock Exchange: see page 95

Grand Central Terminal: see pages 102–3

Woolworth Building: see page 104

Empire State Building: see pages 112–13

Chrysler Building: see page 125

Rockefeller Center: see pages 126–7

HUDSON VALLEY

Lyndhurst: see pages 42–3

Olana: see page 78

ALBANY

State Capitol: 1867–97; the south façade was designed by H.H. Richardson

IRVINGTON

Armour-Stiner House: see page79

ROCHESTER

First Unitarian Church: designed by Louis I. Kahn (1967)

NORTH CAROLINA

ASHEVILLE

Grove Park Inn Resort & Spa: one of the South's oldest resorts, built 1913

EDENTON

North Carolina's first state capital in 1722, features pre-Civil War houses

SOMERSET PLACE STATE HISTORIC SITE

1830s Greek Revival plantation house

FORT MACON STATE PARK

Constructed 1826–34 to the design of French military engineer Simon Bernard

BUXTON

Cape Hatteras Light: see pages 62–5

WILMINGTON

Bellamy Mansion Museum of History and Design Arts: antebellum mansion

Thalian Hall: theater designed by John Montague Trimble, 1858

ASHEVILLE

Biltmore Estate: see pages 88–9

CHAPEL HILL

University of North Carolina: dating from 1789

RALEIGH

North Carolina State Capitol: Greek Revival building by Town and Davis, 1833–40

WINSTON-SALEM

Single Brothers House: built in 1771, a hostel community for unmarried men

Reynolda House Museum of American Art: former home of tobacco baron Richard Joshua Reynolds; designed by Charles Barton Keen

NORTH DAKOTA

WILLISTON

Fort Union Trading Post National Historic Site: originally built by the American Fur Company in 1828

Fort Buford State Historic Site: established in 1866 to protect settlers; Sitting Bull and 200 Sioux surrendered here in 1881

MINOT

Scandinavian Heritage Park: a 225-year old house brought from Norway

STANTON

Knife River Indian Villages National Historic Site: archaeological remains of the Northern Plains Indians, including a Hidatsa earth lodge

WASHBURN

Fort Mandan State Historic Site: 1804–5 fort of Lewis and Clark

FORT CLARK

Fort Clark State Historic Site: built 1831, a major fur trading post

MANDAN

Fort Lincoln State Park: restored Custer House (1874) and earth lodge reconstructions at the site of the On-a-Slant Mandan village (17th century)

BISMARCK

State Capitol: a mid-1930s 19-story Art Deco structure

Cape Hancock State Historic Site: preserves an 1872 military installation

RUGBY

Pioneer Village and Museum 30 reconstructed frontier buildings

WALHALLA

Gingras Trading Post State Historic Site: preserved hand-hewn log home and trading post of Metis fur trader Antoine Gingras, who died in 1877

FORT TOTTEN INDIAN RESERVATION

Fort Totten State Historic Site: buildings of a military post built in 1867

FARGO

Bonanzaville: village of 40 late-19th- and early-20th-century buildings

OHIO

SOUTH BASS ISLAND

Perry's Victory and International Peace Memorial: 352-foot stone Doric column and observation deck at site of the Battle of Lake Erie, 1813

Heineman Winery: the only vineyard that survived Prohibition here

MILAN

Thomas Edison Birthplace: restored 1847 childhood home of the inventor

MENTOR

James A. Garfield National Historic Site: 1876 presidential home

CLEVELAND

Avenue at Tower City: mall with an observation deck on the 42nd floor

Cleveland Union Terminal Tower: 52-story tower built above the Cleveland railroad terminal (1930)

OBERLIN

Oberlin College: America's first co-ed university and one of the first to enroll black students; played an important role in the Underground Railroad

NEW PHILADELPHIA

Schoenbrunn Village State Memorial: reconstructed village founded in 1772 as a Moravian mission

COLUMBUS

Ohio Statehouse: renovated 1839 Greek Revival structure

German Village and Brewery District: mid-19th century settlement of German immigrants

Rock and Roll Hall of Fame: designed by I.M. Pei, 1998

CINCINNATI

MainStrasse Village: 19th-century German neighborhood

Carew Tower: Art Deco building with viewing gallery on its top floor

Taft Museum: an 1820 Federal-style mansion

Cincinnati Museum Center: *see* page 124

OKLAHOMA

NORMAN

Bavinger House: designed by Bruce Goff in 1950, built 1951–55; the design is based on a helix with a spiral form supported by a central mast

MIAMI

Coleman Theater Beautiful: 1929, Spanish Revival style

BARTLESVILLE

Price Tower: designed by Frank Lloyd Wright in 1956 with cantilevered stories resembling the branches of a tall tree

TULSA

Philbrook Museum of Art: a Florentine-style mansion

GUTHRIE

Guthrie Historical District: noted for its restored Victorian architecture

Scottish Rite Masonic Temple: the largest Masonic complex in the world

OKLAHOMA CITY

Oklahoma Theater Center: opened in 1970, designed by John Johansen

OREGON

ASTORIA

Flavel House: 1885 Queen Anne mansion

Heritage Museum: 1904 Classical Revival building, formerly the city hall

Fort Clatsop National Memorial: camp of Lewis and Clark (1805–06)

Fort Stevens State Park: military reservation with fort

NEWPORT

Tillamook County Pioneer Museum: 1905 courthouse

PORTLAND

Old Town Historic District: site of original settlement in 1843

New Market Theater: built in 1875

Pittock Mansion: restored 1914 French Renaissance Revival mansion

Equitable Building: Pietro Belluschi's 1948 structure, known as an example of a "pure glass box"; the first to be sheathed in aluminum, to use double-glazed window panels, and to be sealed and fully air-conditioned

Portland Building: landmark designed by Michael Graves in 1980

SAUVIE ISLAND

Howell Territorial Park: restored mid-19th-century residences

COLUMBIA RIVER GORGE

Fort Dalles Historical Museum: restored 1850 fort

CLACKAMAS COUNTY

Timberline Lodge: *see* page 107

OREGON CITY

Rose Farm: restored 1847 house where the first territorial legislature met

CHAMPOEG STATE PARK

Originally a Calapooya village site, now a log-cabin museum

ALBANY

Monteith House: 1849, Albany's oldest structure

SHANIKO

A ghost town with many remnants of the original settlement preserved

PENDLETON

Pendleton Underground: subterranean passages used during Prohibition

PENNSYLVANIA

HARRISBURG

State Capitol: Theodore Roosevelt called it "the handsomest building I ever saw"; Italian Renaissance style; dome is modeled after St. Peter's in Rome

HERSHEY

Town built in 1903 by candy magnate Milton S Hershey for his chocolate factory; its streets have such names as Chocolate and Cocoa Avenue and streetlamps are in the shape of Hershey's Chocolate Kisses

PHILADELPHIA

Independence Hall: *see* pages 20–21

City Hall: *see* page 60
Museum of American Art: elaborate, multicolored Victorian structure
Eastern State Penitentiary: its Gothic fortifications fill an entire block of the residential neighborhood; opened in 1829
Independence Hall National Park: four blocks of red-brick Georgian and Federal-style buildings
Congress Hall: built in 1787 as the Philadelphia county courthouse
Free Quaker Meeting House: built in 1783 by the small group of Quakers who fought in the Revolutionary War
Pennsylvania Academy of Art: America's oldest art school and museum, designed in an eclectic style
Christ Church: site of worship for Washington, Franklin and Betsy Ross (1727)
Elfreth's Alley: claiming to be the "oldest street in the United States," it has been in continuous residential use since 1727
Society Hill: an residential area of Colonial, Federal and Georgian homes
Second Bank of the U.S.: early 19th-century Greek Revival structure with graceful Ionic columns modeled on the Parthenon in Greece

PITTSBURGH
PPG Place: Philip Johnson's Postmodern black-glass Gothic complex
Point State Park: the 1764 Fort Pitt Blockhouse, the city's oldest structure
Carnegie Science Center: huge state-of-the-art complex opened in 1991
Cathedral of Learning: 42-story Gothic-revival building, called by Frank Lloyd Wright "the world's largest Keep Off the Grass sign"
Heinz Memorial Chapel: French Gothic structure with stained-glass windows
Allegheny County Courthouse: considered by Henry Hobson Richardson to be his best work

DOYLESTOWN
Fonthill: a 44 room "castle" built between 1908 and 1912

ELKINS PARK
Beth Sholom Synagogue: *see* pages 146–7

LANCASTER COUNTY
Amish Barn: *see* page 50

MILL RUN
Fallingwater: *see* pages 140–1

RHODE ISLAND

PROVIDENCE
Rhode Island State Capitol: *see* page 61
Blithewold Mansion, Gardens & Arboretum: turn-of-the-century mansion
Governor Henry Lippitt House Museum: Renaissance Revival mansion (1865)

PAWTUCKET
Slater Mill Historic Site: textile-manufacturing buildings (1750s to 1810s)

WARWICK
Apponaug Village: settled in 1696; 18th- and 19th-century structures, including Warwick City Hall, a Victorian-era building with a clock tower
Pawtuxet Village: settled in 1642, claims to be New England's oldest village

BRISTOL
Linden Place: Federal mansion designed in 1810

EAST GREENWICH
General James Mitchell Varnum House Museum: 1773 Federal mansion

NEWPORT
Old Colony House: pre-Revolutionary brick building; seat of government from 1739 to 1900
Touro Synagogue National Historic Site: dedicated in 1762, the oldest synagogue in the United States
Trinity Church: 1726 colonial structure based on the Old North Church in Boston and the designs of Sir Christopher Wren
Beechwood: 1890s summer home of William Backhouse and Mrs. Astor
Marble House: lavish summer house, built 1888–92 for the Vanderbilts
Rosecliff: 1902 house modeled after the Grand Trianon at Versailles, France
Kingscote: an 1839–41 Arts and Crafts cottage with the earliest known installation of Tiffany glass
The Breakers: *see* pages 90–1
Hammersmith Farm: John F. Kennedy's 28-room summer home
Belcourt Castle: French-style castle, built in Louis XIII style, 1894
Chepstow: Italianate-style villa designed in 1860
The Elms: modeled after the mid-18th century Parisian chateau d'Asnieres; completed in 1901
Isaac Bell House: built in 1883 by McKim, Mead and White
Rose Island Lighthouse: built in 1869
Fort Adams State Park: largest coastal fortification in the United States; an engineering and architectural masterpiece constructed 1824–c.1854

JAMESTOWN
Beavertail Lighthouse Museum: site of the third-oldest lighthouse on the Atlantic coast

SOUTH CAROLINA

CHARLESTON
Historic District: lined with tall, narrow multicolored stucco houses adorned with wooden shutters and ironwork balconies
Drayton Hall: Georgian mansion, built 1738–42
Magnolia Plantation and Gardens: most notable for its ornamental gardens
Fort Sumter National Monument: *see* page 40

GEORGETOWN
Historic District: fine antebellum and 18th-century houses
Belle W. Baruch Plantation
Hopsewee Plantation
Hampton Plantation State Park: 18th-century Neoclassical monolith built by Huguenots
Boone Hall Plantation: from the late 17th century but the house is a 20th-century reconstruction; grounds include a slave street of small brick cabins that housed privileged slaves—domestic servants and skilled artisans

ST. HELENA ISLAND
Penn Center National Historic District: includes the Gullah Institute, a school for freed slaves, and a retreat for civil rights leaders in the 1960s

SOUTH DAKOTA

STURGIS
Old Fort Meade Museum: established 1878 after the Battle of Little Bighorn

DEADWOOD
Infamous "Wild West" Gold Rush town, and a National Historic Landmark
Historic Franklin Hotel: constructed in 1903
Saloon No.10: where Wild Bill Hickock was shot and killed by Jack McCall

WALL
Wall Drug: world-famous emporium, begun in 1931

MOBRIDGE
Sherr Howe Arena: contains 10 murals of Sioux artist Oscar Howe, painted in 1942, depicting the life of the Plains Indians

HURON
Pyle House Museum: built in 1894, still with original fixtures; former residence of Gladys Pyle, the 1st Republican woman elected to the US senate

MITCHELL
Corn Palace: Moorish structure, built in 1892 to encourage settlement and display agricultural products; decorated with murals fashioned of corn

DE SMET
Little Town on the Prairie: made famous by author Laura Ingalls Wilder

SISSETON
Joseph N. Nicollet Tower and Interpretive Center: 75-foot tower

SIOUX FALLS
Historic District: contains the city's oldest, grandest mansions

TENNESSEE

KNOXVILLE

World's Fair Park: dominated by the futuristic Sunsphere, a glass ball mounted on a round concrete tower, with an observation deck on its lower level

FRANKLIN

Carnton Plantation: a former Confederate hospital

LYNCHBURG

Jack Daniel's Distillery: founded in 1866, the oldest registered distillery in the U.S.

MEMPHIS

Beale Street Historic District: rebuilt with 1920s façades
Hunt–Phelan Home: completed in 1832, antebellum home
Graceland: home of Elvis Presley
Memphis Pink Palace Museum and Planetarium: centers on the pink marble mansion of Clarence Saunders, who founded America's first chain of self-service supermarkets, Piggly-Wiggly, in 1916
National Civil Rights Museum: built around the remains of the Lorraine Motel, where Dr. Martin Luther King, Jr., was assassinated in 1968
Pyramid: surreal 32-story, 321-foot structure, two-thirds the size of the Great Pyramid, and taller than the Statue of Liberty; completed in 1991, it was intended as a symbolic link with the Nile Delta

NASHVILLE

Fort Nashborough: reconstruction of the original fort of 1779
Grand Old Opry: the name of America's longest-running radio show, which moved in 1943 to a former tabernacle, the *Ryman Auditorium*

TEXAS

DALLAS

Thanksgiving Square
Morton H. Meyerson Symphony Center: designed by I. M. Pei
West End Historic District: site of the original 1841 settlement on Lamar and Munger Streets
Texas Schoolbook Depository: now the Dallas County Administration Building
Reunion Tower (*see* page 162)

FORT WORTH

"Wall Street of the West": the Fort Worth Livestock Exchange

FREDERICKSBURG

Nimitz Steamboat Hotel: once the last hotel on the road to California

AUSTIN

Capitol Complex: comprises more than two dozen state government offices, including the Texas State Capitol (1888)
Governor's Mansion: constructed 1856
East 6th Street: thoroughfare with buildings dating from the 19th century

SAN ANTONIO

King William Historic District: 19th-century homes of German merchants.
Tower of the Americas: observation deck at 750 feet
San Fernando Cathedral: the oldest cathedral in the United States
Spanish Governors Palace: home to Spanish officials during the mission era
The Alamo: *see* page 18

CADDOAN MOUNDS STATE HISTORIC SITE

Site of the Caddo Indians, an early Southeastern mound-building culture

ABILENE

Paramount Theatre: with elaborate Moorish interior

EL PASO

Ysleta del Sur: the oldest mission in the United States, established 1692

HOUSTON

Astrodome: the first ballpark to have a roof over its playing field (1966)
Pennzoil Place: built in 1976, the twin 36-story towers are separated only by a narrow 10-foot vertical slot
Fred Hartman Bridge: *see* pages 182–3

UTAH

LOGAN

LDS Temple: built in 1877, the oldest still in use anywhere

BRIGHAM CITY

Box Elder Tabernacle: rebuilt after a fire of 1896, a distinguished example of Mormon architecture

OGDEN

Peery's Egyptian Theater: example of the Egyptian-Revival style (1920s)

SALT LAKE CITY

Capitol Hill: includes the 1915 State Capitol
Commercial Club: Renaissance Revival structure, built 1908
The Avenues Historic District: contains more than 2,000 buildings representing a variety of architectural styles
Temple Square: *see* pages 56–9
Union Pacific Station: *see* page 99

HOVENWEEP NATIONAL MONUMENT

Anasazi ruins, including Hovenweep Castle, constructed around AD 1200

VERMONT

MONTPELIER

State Capitol: built in 1859 in the Renaissance Revival style, with a dome

WATERBURY

Ben & Jerry's Ice Cream Factory: tours of the famous company feature a short film, an observation platform, and a free scoop!

WHITE RIVER JUNCTION

Hotel Coolidge: an authentic railroad hotel, still open for guests

WOODSTOCK

Marsh-Billings-Rockefeller National Historical Park

PLYMOUTH NOTCH

President Calvin Coolidge State Historic Site: birthplace and boyhood home

WINDSOR

The Old Constitution House

MANCHESTER

Hildene: 1902 stately summer home built by Robert Todd Lincoln

BRATTLEBORO

Naulakha: Shingle Style house, designed by Rudyard Kipling in 1892–93
Old Railroad Station: opened 1849

VIRGINIA

ARLINGTON

The Pentagon: the headquarters of the US military establishment

CHARLOTTESVILLE

University of Virginia: in 1976 the university was officially designated the greatest piece of architecture in the U.S., designed by Thomas Jefferson
Monticello: *see* page 23

FREDERICKSBURG

Gunston Hall: 1755 home designed by William Buckland

COLONIAL WILLIAMSBURG

Opened in 1934, with restored buildings re-creating colonial trades

JAMESTOWN NATIONAL HISTORIC SITE

The first successful English colony in the New World, dating from 1607; a 50-foot tower of the first brick church, built in 1639, remains

RICHMOND

Church Hill: one of the town's oldest surviving residential districts
Virginia State Capitol: the seat of the state government,
White House of the Confederacy: a Neoclassical mansion where Jefferson Davis lived as Confederate president
Monument Avenue: lined with c.1900 mansions; laid out by city planners from 1889 to commemorate key figures of the Confederacy
Poe Museum: the town's oldest building, a 250-year-old stone house

CHANTILLY
Dulles Airport: designed by Eero Saarinen (1958–62)
FAIRFAX COUNTY
Mount Vernon: *see* page 22

WASHINGTON

SEATTLE
Coliseum Theater: opened in 1916 as Seattle's first motion picture theater
Experience Music Project: designed by Frank Gehry in 2000; features no right angles on its exterior; each of its 21,000 shingles has a unique shape
Smith Tower: *see* page 105
Space Needle: *see* pages 154–5
TACOMA
Fort Nisqually Historic Site: 1833 fort built by the Hudson's Bay Company
OYSTERVILLE
Fort Canby State Park: features the oldest lighthouse in the Pacific Northwest
VANCOUVER
Fort Vancouver National Historic Site: the original fort was largely destroyed by 1866; there is now a reconstructed stockade with chief factor's house
GOLDENDALE
Maryhill Museum of Art: *see* pages 138–9
GRAND COULEE DAM
The largest single producer of electricity in the United States; completed 1942
SPOKANE
Spokane County Courthouse: Chateauesque-style 1895 structure
Fort Spokane: the last frontier army post in the Pacific Northwest
DAYTON
Dayton Historical Depot: oldest existing railroad station in the state
Columbia County Courthouse: oldest courthouse in Washington
WALLA WALLA
Fort Walla Walla Museum Complex: contains a small pioneer village of 16 original and replica structures dating from 1859
PORT TOWNSEND
Manresa Castle: built 1892 for a prominent member of the community

WEST VIRGINIA

LEWISBURG
Originally a frontier outpost during the Indian Wars of the 1770s
WHITE SULPHUR SPRINGS
The Greenbrier: originally built 1780, the grandest hotel in West Virginia
CASS
An old lumber-mill village, preserved in its entirety as a historic park
CHARLESTON
State Capitol: golden-domed edifice, designed by Cass Gilbert, 1932
HARPERS FERRY
An 18th-century town restored as a national historic park
BERKELEY SPRINGS
Preserved as a state historic park, it was a favorite spa and summer retreat of the colonial elite; the old Roman Baths, have been in active use since 1815
Berkeley Castle: a fortresslike mid-Victorian folly
FAYETTEVILLE
New River Gorge Bridge: a single-span steel arch that rises 900 feet above a spectacular river canyon; 4,224 feet long, it was completed in 1978
HINTON
A purpose-built company railroad town, dating from about 1900

WISCONSIN

WIND POINT
Wingspread: designed by Frank Lloyd Wright in 1937; a unique Prairie house, oriented so that the sunlight falls in all rooms
MILWAUKEE
Pabst Mansion: completed in 1892; lavish home of a brewing baron
Annunciation Greek Orthodox Church: a 1956 design of Frank Lloyd Wright
Villa Terrace Decorative Arts Museum: Italian Renaissance mansion
MADISON
State Capitol: sumptuous white granite structure, built 1906–17
Unitarian Meeting House: Frank Lloyd Wright structure; late 1940s
Monona Terrace Community and Convention Center: a Frank Lloyd Wright design
SPRING GREEN
Home to Frank Lloyd Wright's *Taliesin* and *Hillside Home School*
House on the Rock: built by Alex Jordan from 1944, on and of a natural 60-foot chimneylike rock; never lived in, it is a labyrinth of low ceilings, indoor pools, waterfalls, and trees
RACINE
Johnson Wax Building: *see* pages 142–3

WYOMING

CASPER
Nicolaysen Museum: housed in a disused power station
CHEYENNE
Historic Governor's Mansion: Georgian Revival brick residence with Corinthian portico; home of the nation's first woman governor
State Capitol: seat of government since 1888, dominated by Corinthian columned pavilions and a gold-leafed dome; interior is embellished with murals depicting Wyoming's history
Union Pacific Depot: sprawling Richardsonian Romanesque structure of 1887
ENCAMPMENT
Grand Encampment Museum: preserves a number of buildings from the 1890s copper mining town
FORT BRIDGER
The second permanent white settlement in Wyoming, established in 1842; reconstruction of the log fort with blacksmith's and carpenter's shops
SOUTH PASS CITY STATE HISTORIC SITE
A gold rush ghost town, deserted by 1875; 24 original buildings are preserved, including the South Pass Hotel of 1868
CASPER
Fort Caspar: reconstructed fortification of 1862
FORT LARAMIE NATIONAL HISTORIC SITE
The earliest permanent white settlement in Wyoming, built in 1834 as a fur trading post, and subsequently abandoned in 1890; eleven structures are restored to their historic appearance
YELLOWSTONE NATIONAL PARK
Old Faithful Inn: stands beside the world's most famous geyser; built of rocks and lodgepole pines in Western Stick style from 1903–28; the open lobby rises more than 90 feet, edged with branch railings and log staircases
RIVERTON
Saint Stephen's Mission: began in 1884, the permanent structures date from 1887, including the church, which is painted inside and out with bright Arapaho geometric designs
CODY
Buffalo Bill Historical Center: includes his boyhood home, built 1841 and moved here in 1933
Irma Hotel: Buffalo Bill's famous hotel, built 1902 to accommodate big-game hunters on their way to Yellowstone; it is adorned with a stone buffalo head above the corner entrance
SHERIDAN
Sheridan Inn: built 1893 by the General Manager of the Chicago, Burlington & Quincy Railroad, a gambrel-roofed hotel with many dormers, supposedly modeled on a Scottish country inn

BIBLIOGRAPHY

Andrews, Wayne. *Architecture in America: A Photographic History from the Colonial Period to the Present,* rev. ed. N.Y.: Atheneum, 1979,

Blumenson, John J.G. *Identifying American Architecture: A Pictorial Guide to Styles and Terms, 1600-1945,* 2nd ed. N.Y.: W.W. Norton, 1981.

Bowman, John S., ed. *The World Almanac of the American West.* N.Y.: Pharos Books, 1986.

Carley, Rachel. *The Visual Dictionary of American Domestic Architecture,* illus. Ray Skibinski and Ed Lam. N.Y.: Henry Holt, 1994.

Daley, Les, and Mark S. Wexler. "Get Muddy, Save a Church," *Smithsonian,* Jan 2000.

Folsom, Merrill. *Great American Mansions and Their Stories.* Mamaroneck, N.Y.: Hastings House, 1963.

Goldberger, Paul. *The Skyscraper.* N.Y.: Alfred A. Knopf, 1981.

Gowans, Alan. *Images of American Living: Four Centuries of Architecture and Furniture As Cultural Expression.* Phila.: J.B. Lippincott, 1964.

Headley, Gwyn. *Architectural Follies in America.* N.Y.: John Wiley & Sons, 1996.

Huxtable, Ada Louise. *The Tall Building Artistically Reconsidered: The Search for a Skyscraper Style.* N.Y.: Pantheon Books, 1982.

Lacayo, Richard. "Mies Is More," *Time,* June 25, 2001.

Newhouse, Elizabeth L., ed. *The Builders: Marvels of Engineering.* Wash., DC: The National Geographic Society, 1992.

Rifkind, Carole. *A Field Guide to American Architecture.* N.Y.: New American Library Div., Penguin Books USA, 1980.

Stern, Robert A.M., with Thomas Mellins and Raymond Gastil. *Pride of Place: Building the American Dream.* Boston: Houghton Mifflin; and N.Y.: American Heritage, 1986.

U.S. Library of Congress. "Historic American Buildings Survey," various authors/dates. Washington, DC.

GLOSSARY

adobe: Sun-dried clay bricks used for building in warm, dry climates; also "puddled adobe," wet clay applied over such bricks as a protective coating and renewed regularly.

appliqué: An ornament fastened to the surface or interior of a building.

arcade: A passageway with a roof supported by arched columns.

balustrade: A row of miniature columns (balusters) supporting a handrail, often used decoratively to frame or crown porches.

Baroque: A post-Renaissance style characterized by ornate decoration, curvaceous forms, and complex compositions.

buttress: A masonry pier used for reinforcement of structural walls.

capital: The top part of a column, usually decorated, and larger than the column shaft.

cantilever: A projecting beam that is supported at only one end to form, for example, a balcony.

cladding: A finishing material, such as boards, shingles, or metal, overlaid on an unfinished wall or roof as weather-proofing.

colonnade: A row of columns with horizontal entablature, such as friezes or sculptures, above.

cornice: A projecting feature, usually decorative, at the top of walls, arches, and eaves.

curtain wall: A wall made entirely of glass framed by steel or other supporting materials.

crenellations: Notched rooflines of medieval origin, also called battlements for their original defensive function.

dormer: An upright window that projects from a sloping roof; may be gabled, shedlike, circular, etc., depending upon building style.

eaves: The lower edge of a roof that projects beyond the wall below.

finial: A vertical ornament fixed to the peak of an arch or rooftop.

frieze: A decorative band around the top of a wall.

gable: The triangular area enclosed by the edges of a sloping roof. The gable ends of a building are the walls under the gables (usually at the sides); the eave ends are the walls below the faces of a sloping roof.

half-timbering: A type of timber-frame construction in which the surfaces between post and beam supports are filled in with another material, leaving part of the timber visible on the building's surface.

jetty: A second-story projection over the first-story façade often seen in medieval-style buildings.

Mansard roof: One having a double slope on all four sides, the lower slope being steeper than the upper, as seen in buildings of the French Empire style (named for the 17th-century French architect François Mansard).

ogee arch: An arch of two curves meeting at a point, as in Eastern architecture; also, a double curve with the shape of an elongated S.

order: columns or pilasters in various Greco-Roman styles, including Doric, Ionic, and Corinthian.

parapet: A low wall or railing along the edge of a roof or balcony.

pilaster: Shallow pier attached to a wall, usually column-shaped or rectangular, for decoration and/or reinforcement.

siding: Boards, shingles, or other material used to surface a frame building.

span: The length of a bridge from the beginning to the end of the structure.

stickwork: The exterior patterned woodwork that serves an ornamental rather than a structural purpose; widely used on Victorian-style houses.

stucco: A durable finish for exterior walls, usually composed of cement, sand, and lime.

vault: An arched (domed) roof or ceiling.